Read Well, Think Well

Read Well, Think Well

Build Your Child's **Reading, Comprehension, and Critical-Thinking Skills**

Hal W. Lanse, PhD

Avon, Massachusetts

Published by
Adams Media, an F+W Publications Company
57 Littlefield Street, Avon, MA 02322. U.S.A.
www.adamsmedia.com

ISBN-10: 1-59869-782-X
ISBN-13: 978-1-59869-782-7

Printed in the United States of America.

J I H G F E D C B A

Library of Congress Cataloging-in-Publication Data
is available from the publisher.

This publication is designed to provide accurate and authoritative information
with regard to the subject matter covered. It is sold with the understanding
that the publisher is not engaged in rendering legal, accounting, or other
professional advice. If legal advice or other expert assistance is required, the
services of a competent professional person should be sought.
—From a *Declaration of Principles* jointly adopted by a Committee of the
American Bar Association and a Committee of Publishers and Associations

Many of the designations used by manufacturers and sellers to distinguish
their product are claimed as trademarks. Where those designations appear
in this book and Adams Media was aware of a trademark claim, the designations have been printed with initial capital letters.

This book is available at quantity discounts for bulk purchases.
For information, please call 1-800-289-0963.

This book is dedicated to my parents, Bernice and Jerome Lanse, who filled my childhood with books and set me on the path to becoming a teacher and author. This book is also for my grandfather, Harry Saunders, for the endless supply of comic books that helped set my youthful imagination on fire.

Contents

At Long Last: A **Training Manual** for Parents

Kids don't come with an owner's manual. Right? We've all heard it and most of us believe it. There are no easy answers to many of life's challenges—and parenting is one of the greatest challenges of all. So it might surprise you to know that when it comes to reading there *are* answers. Scientific answers. Research-based answers. Learning to read and to think critically about books is not a matter of luck and it's not a matter of genetics. Your child can learn to read; what's more, *you* can (and must) become your child's best teacher. That's right: The power to change your child's educational future lies with you. I have the knowledge and the expertise to show you how to make it happen.

For generations, our nation has had a crisis in reading. Today, getting kids to read is more critical than ever. Manufacturing jobs have gone overseas and the void has been filled by jobs that require dramatically elevated levels of literacy and intellectual flexibility. Under the No Child Left Behind Act of 2001, the federal law designed to improve primary and secondary school education, slow progress has begun, but schools can't do it alone.

My fellow parents, I say to you: We all have to help. We have to become actively involved in our children's education if they are to succeed in life. No matter how well your local school functions, nothing can replace the support and guidance that you can provide. If your local school is not functioning well, then your help is needed even more. I can assist you. This book contains a series of strategies that can transform children, at any age, into skilled readers and critical thinkers.

Parents, I say to you: Your kids are already smart. You just need the techniques to unlock their potential. I'll teach them to you. Teachers, I say to you: If you want to join the battle, learn the same strategies and use them in your classroom.

No Child Left Behind recognizes parental involvement as a key factor in educational success. The U.S. Department of Education's *Parental Involvement Report* tells us:

> Three decades of research provide convincing evidence that parents are an important influence in helping their children achieve high academic standards. When schools collaborate with parents to help their children learn and when parents participate in school activities and decision-making about their children's education, children achieve at higher levels. In short, when parents are involved in education, children do better in school.

Parental involvement is more than just checking homework and more than just reading aloud. There are many activities that can support learning. You can prepare your child for success practically from infancy. The most successful school children enter school prepared by their parents and they continue to get parental support throughout their school years.

The U.S. Department of Education tells us:

> By the age of four, children from higher socio-economic families have been exposed to 45 million words, whereas children from lower socio-economic families have only been exposed to 13 million words. These differences in exposure to language through parent-child interactions during early childhood have a strong influence on later reading and school achievement.

While it is true that children from middle-class and wealthy families do better in school, this does not mean that all middle-class children do well. A review of Department of Education statistics tells us that in every state of the union, 50 percent or higher of children from all backgrounds fail to achieve reading proficiency. One can speculate on why this problem affects even the well-to-do. Perhaps increased time at work and less time spent with family affects many children of privilege. Maybe it's the stress of modern living that interferes with learning. You will learn much in this book about the dangers of childhood stress and how to handle it. Whatever the reason, one thing is clear. American children from all walks of life are struggling with reading and critical thinking.

The more support a child gets at home, the more proficient she'll become at reading and at learning in general. All families from all backgrounds can benefit from the knowledge contained in this book. Schools are important, but make no mistake about it: Parental support or the lack of it has far-reaching consequences.

In April 2000, the National Reading Panel released a report that identified the five key abilities of effective reading instruction. They are:

1. Phonemic awareness
2. Phonics
3. Fluency
4. Growing vocabulary
5. Comprehension

Briefly, *phonemic awareness* is the ability to hear the sounds and sound combinations. The term *phonics* refers to the explicit teaching of the connection between sounds and written symbols (letters and letter combinations). For example, phonics teaches that the *c* in *cat* is pronounced differently from the *c* in *face* and that the *e* in *face*, while silent, influences the pronunciation of the word.

Fluency is the ability to read a passage smoothly, easily, and with expression. A fluent reader recognizes the rise and fall and changes of tone in a reading passage. *Vocabulary instruction*, the National Reading Panel tells us, should be taught both directly, in school vocabulary exercises, and indirectly, through lots of childhood experiences reading interesting stories and learning about the world. In this book you will learn a lot about how to give your child a wide knowledge of the world and, consequently, a broad vocabulary. This will benefit your child at every stage of life up to and including college.

Comprehension is a reader's ability to understand the meaning of a book, a play, an article, a poem. This is a very complex human skill involving many different types of thinking processes. Many parents are familiar with programs that address the first two topics listed above: phonemic awareness and phonics. Programs like Hooked on Phonics do a great job developing these skills. There are far fewer resources available to parents who want to build vocabulary, fluency, and comprehension skills. That's where I come in. *Read Well, Think Well* is for parents—and teachers—who want to help children build vocabulary, fluency, and comprehension.

Gone are the days when a youngster could leave high school and support a family by going to work in a factory. Today, the ability to read critically is a basic economic necessity—a survival skill. An unwritten rule of modern American economics is "read well or starve." Ours is a knowledge economy, one that stresses the finding and disseminating of information rather than the manufacturing of goods. High-level reading is now an entry-level skill.

How important is the need to read well and become highly educated? In 2002, the U.S. Census Bureau issued a report in which it said:

Over the past 25 years, earnings differences have grown among workers with different levels of educational attainment . . . full-time, year-round workers with a bachelor's degree had 1.5 times the annual earnings of workers with only a high school diploma. By 1999, this ratio had risen to 1.8. Workers with an advanced degree, who earned 1.8 times the earnings of high school graduates in 1975, averaged 2.6 times the earnings of workers with a high school diploma in 1999. During the same period, the relative earnings of the least educated workers fell. While in 1975, full-time, year-round workers without a high school diploma earned 0.9 times the earnings of workers with a high school diploma; by 1999, they were earning only 0.7 times the average earnings of high school graduates.

Good reading skills must be cultivated from the earliest age. Reading is the key to higher education. Without higher education, your child's lifetime earnings will be much smaller—some experts say by as much as a million dollars! Without good reading skills, your child will likely be condemned to a life of poverty or at best a life of struggle.

As a single parent, I stand in empathy and solidarity with all other parents. I know the future can be better for America's children and I'm doing my best to help. Failure is not inevitable; neither is economic instability. The future can be bright for our children, and reading well is a legacy we can offer them. All he needs is a few good books and you—armed with knowledge. If your child can read well and think well, he can achieve anything. I'm here to help!

—Hal W. Lanse

CHAPTER 1

The Big Six: The **Key Comprehension Skills** That Your Child *Must* Master

If your child is in second grade or higher, her teacher might tell you that she's reading well. As a concerned parent, you must then ask, "What do you mean by reading well?" It's quite possible that you will be told one of the following:

"She can decode most of the words."

"Her phonics skills are great."

"She pronounces the words well when she reads aloud."

It's true, most children in general education classes are pretty good at these skills. But this doesn't mean they can read! Reading is more than phonics. It's more than decoding. Reading is also about understanding, or what literacy experts call *comprehension*. Guess what? Most teachers don't teach comprehension. For the past twenty-five years researchers have noted that children comprehend the basic plot elements of stories but go bust when it comes to the deeper meanings. Most children cannot grasp these deeper meanings on their own. It's not a matter of intelligence. Our kids aren't stupid. Comprehension must be explicitly taught and most educators are not trained to teach it. In fact, many teachers that I've trained over the years had no idea that they *weren't* teaching comprehension. It's not their fault. In the age of test-prep we've confused drilling kids with instruction. They aren't the same.

If your local school gives lots of practice tests throughout the year, your child is being robbed of precious instructional time. Don't get me wrong. I'm not against assessment, but I'm an advocate of *smart* assessments. Smart assessments are brief and they don't require teachers to sit their students down for lengthy, complicated, stressful tests. Most assessments can be done with a conversation while the teacher is jotting down some brief and focused notes.

I'll teach you how to do it. It's not complicated. You don't have to spend years at your local teachers' college to learn. As your child's most important teacher you can learn the six key competencies of reading instruction, and you can learn how to teach them to your child.

Here are the Big Six:

1. Predicting
2. Questioning the text
3. Using text features
4. Hearing the text
5. Visualizing the text
6. Summarizing

None of these competencies is more important than the others, nor do they go in any particular order. Teaching any one of these will bring your child's reading comprehension a long way. Work on one until he's good at it, then work on another.

Number 1: Predicting

Good readers build theories in their heads. They think, "I believe the character is going to (run away from home) because he's already said (he wants to join the circus and get away from his battling parents)." (The parentheses get filled in with the particular details of a story.) The prediction, even in sophisticated adult readers, is sometimes correct and sometimes not. Being incorrect doesn't make you a bad reader. Having no theory at all makes you a bad reader. Good readers, even very young ones, develop theories as they read; and very often they revisit their theories. A good reader might say, "Ha, I was right! When the hero said (the planet Xenon must be saved), I knew he was going to (steal his father's star cruiser and join the intergalactic army)." The same good reader might also say, "Oh, my theory can't be right. Now that the author has told me that (the hero is blind), I know that my prediction that the character will (steal the star cruiser) can't be true. But now that I know that (he's always talking his best friend into doing crazy things) I'm thinking that maybe the hero will (talk his friend into stealing the star cruiser and joining him on the adventure)."

See? A good reader makes theories, then checks and revises them. So how do you teach a young reader to think like this? Easy. You show him how *you* do it. Read a story together with your child. Read it aloud while he follows along. Stop every now and then and say, "I'm noticing that the character said (she hates asparagus) and that the family (always feeds scraps to the dog). I'm thinking that maybe later in the story she's going to (give the asparagus to Rover). Let's read on and check. Aha! I was right!" or "Wait a second! *Now* she's saying that (Rover hates vegetables too), so I was wrong. My new prediction is that (she's going to toss the asparagus into the trash masher) because now I'm noticing that (the family is talking a lot about their beautiful new trash masher)."

The more skilled your child gets, the more he can be challenged. If he gets really good at predicting and revising predictions about what characters will do, you can try some more-sophisticated predictions. This will require that you tap into your child's growing understanding of the patterns in stories.

Some of these patterns are:

Problem/solution: "I know that in books there's often a problem that a character or group of characters has to solve. I noticed that in this book (the character is afraid of heights). But I also noticed the fact that (he loves his Dad, with whom he is on a trip in the mountains). This makes me think that maybe the character is going to (overcome his fear of heights) by (saving his Dad from an accident on the mountain top)."

A life lesson: "I noticed that the author said that (playing with fire is dangerous). I think the author is going to teach the reader a life lesson by having the heroine (cause a fire); then she'll learn (the error of her ways when she sees the harm she has done to her sister's new condo)."

Characters change: "I noticed that the character has been (saying bad things about black people). I also noticed that (an African American ambulance driver moved in next door). As a result, I think the character is going to change (when the driver saves him or somebody he loves)."

There are similar books in this genre: "I noticed that in biographies the person being written about usually (overcomes a personal difficulty to become an achiever). I think that in this book the difficulty is (the fact that she was blind and still wanted to win the Olympics)." The same type of pattern can be looked for in mysteries (the detective has a special skill, job, or personality trait that helps her solve the crime) and in science fiction stories (evil is threatening the world and someone who doesn't see himself as a hero has to save the day).

There are other books by this author: "I've read a couple of other books by this author. In her books the main character always (finds an eccentric adult who can teach her to love her own uniqueness). I think maybe in this book (she'll learn from her Harley-riding grandmother)."

Remember, in all of these cases you're modeling your own thinking for your child. Gradually, after a few books, try to turn the modeling into a shared conversation. "Oh my gosh, the hero just said that (he dreamed his twin sister is *still alive* and calling to him from the Haunted Zone). What do you think he's going to do?"

Always have the experience be fun and relaxed. *Never grill your child.* Research indicates that if reading becomes stressful, electrical impulses shift away from the brain's learning center and toward the brain's self-defense center. It then becomes physically impossible for your child to develop greater comprehension. Learning and stress are mutually and biologically exclusive.

Number 2: Questioning the Text

By predicting, you've already begun questioning the text. When a reader develops a theory and later confirms or revises that theory, she is questioning the text. ("I believe that the trapeze artist must have killed the bearded lady because he's the only person with the ability to fling himself through a second story window.") ("Oh wait, the trapeze artist was in love with her but the lion tamer is really her brother and second in line to inherit the family fortune. Maybe Mr. Big Cat, her brother, is the killer.") There are additional ways that a good reader questions the text:

- Where am I in the story? I lost my train of thought.
- What does the author want me to learn? How do I know?
- Does the author have a particular point of view that others might not have?
- Is the author trying to control my thinking with tricky language?
- Is the author trying to control my thinking by leaving out information?
- Does the author's opinion or facts go along with what I know about the world?

Where Am I in the Story? I Lost My Train of Thought.

Admit it. You're squirming right now. This has happened to you, hasn't it? Relax. It happens to all of us. Not to worry. Lack of sleep, stress, and hunger can all contribute to this problem. And usually it's temporary. But young readers lose their train of thought for another reason. No one teaches them how to hang on to their train of thought. If they're natural readers, swell. If not, they're in trouble.

There are two easy solutions to this problem. It's called *stickies and fingers*. Not to be confused with sticky fingers. That's a totally different problem and you'll just have to go out and buy moist wipes.

Let's start with stickies. You've probably got some on your refrigerator right now. Yeah, *those*. The adhesive pads on which you put your shopping list? They can help your child read. Go to the store and buy the little ones. You may find the ones shaped like arrows to be particularly helpful.

Have your child trace one idea through the book using the stickies. For example, every time you learn something about the main character's feelings, put a sticky on that spot in the book. After your child has read a chapter, have her look back at the stickies and say what she noticed at each spot. Then, a day or so later, when she's ready to read another chapter, have her skim through the stickies from all of the previous chapters, saying what she remembered. Literacy experts call this *accumulating text*, a fancy way of saying practicing remembering.

Begin by doing this with your child. Show her how you use the stickies. Later on, let her try it on her own.

Another way of accumulating text is to use five fingers. Each time your child reads a chapter, have her practice saying the most important events by checking them off across five fingers. Typically, children say too much. When trying to summarize, they spit out every minor incident in the story and mention every minor detail. Together, you and your child can practice boiling down the events of the last chapter, or the story thus far in five clear points. It's not as easy as it sounds. A lot of adults can't do it, so give your kid time.

Another problem you might encounter is that your child neglects to name the important characters when retelling the story. Practice this, too. For further practice, you can make a game of summarizing what the two of you did at the mall, at grandma's house, in the park, and so on. The better your child becomes at retelling events, the better a reader and thinker she'll be.

Number 3: Using Text Features

Parents love to buy books for kids. For the younger ones, it's picture books, fairy tales, and simple chapter books. For older kids there are all sorts of novels: fantasy, mystery, science fiction, adventure stories. Sometimes parents worry that letting kids read fiction will give them a distorted picture of reality. However, a more common feeling is that passionate young readers are very creative in all sorts of ways, and they tend to be quite self-confident, too.

Children who immerse themselves in novels grow up to be creative problem-solvers. Look for a person who has developed a new solution to an old problem and you're likely to find an avid reader—and you'll be able to trace the habit back to childhood.

Reading novels is great for kids, but it isn't enough. They also need exposure to nonfiction—lots of it. There are truckloads of research to show that kids who are exposed to lots of different facts about the world are better readers. Why? Because comprehension involves not just the skill of reading, but knowledge of the countless facts and references that one finds in books, magazines, and newspapers. It's what the literacy gurus call *background knowledge.*

There are many ways to build background knowledge. There are the fancy and formal ways—trips to museums and the theater. And remember that old saying, "Children should be seen and not heard?" *Fuggetaboutit!* If you want a smart kid, baptize him in rivers of conversation. The more things you talk about—ordinary everyday stuff—the more background knowledge your child will have, and the better he'll be at the complex craft of reading.

An easy way to build background knowledge is through nonfiction books. You can buy them from the bookstore or borrow them from the library; you can even ask your child's teacher for sources of catalogues of children's literature. Most companies would be delighted to send you a free catalogue if you call their toll-free number or visit their Web site.

Sit down with your child and order as many books as you can afford. If you can't afford many, see if other parents will share the cost. Then trade among yourselves. And talk. If you and your child read about trucks, talk about the trucks you see on your way to the shopping center. Talk about the roads, the blacktop, the workmen, everything! If you're reading about the weather, talk about words like *precipitation* and *humidity.* Look for every opportunity to chat about the world. It will broaden your child's knowledge base and will provide the fringe benefit (not a small one) of bringing you closer together.

Reading nonfiction brings with it a particular set of opportunities. These books often have parts to them that are designed to build comprehension. But these parts become meaningless blips on your child's radar if he's not taught how to interpret them. You've seen them yourself in magazines and newspapers. They're called *text features.* I'm talking about titles and subsections, illustrations and the captions below them, insets and sidebars. Some of them help you understand the main text; others (often sidebars) add additional information. They're almost like mini-articles within an article.

They're there to make reading more interesting and understandable, but if your child doesn't know it, then text features will be as important to him as a jelly stain on the kitchen floor. (And you know he'll ignore *that*.)

Again, modeling is the key. Show your child how you use text features. I'll give an example. Last week, I visited a middle school special education teacher in her classroom. She was spinning her wheels trying to get her seventh-graders to find the main idea of a nonfiction article. It wasn't happening. She was frustrated and the kids were getting antsy.

Dr. Lanse to the rescue. I picked up a book from the classroom library. Its chapters were formatted much like the article the kids were reading (or not, as it were). I selected a chapter and showed the class the title, a little blurb (summarizing introduction), an illustration, and then demonstrated that, taken together, they told me what the chapter was about. I then read the chapter aloud and stopped and pointed out each fact that illustrated the main idea.

"Okay," I said, "Now do the same thing in your own article." They got it. The teacher was thrilled. The kids were proud. The students already knew they were supposed to find the main idea—a common refrain heard among teachers—but until I demonstrated a procedure for doing it they didn't know how.

Make this a shared experience with your own child. Before starting a nonfiction book, magazine piece, or newspaper article, try to look at all the parts outside the main text. Verbalize for your child what you know about the text before you begin reading. While you're reading, discover together how captions, illustrations, insets, and the like clarify the ideas in the text.

One time, I was visiting a third-grade class. It was independent reading time. Elijah, who loves all things creepy and crawly, was reading a book about insects. There was an illustration of a fly, gloriously detailed and colored. Set into one corner of this illustration was another. Elijah had no idea what this inset was about. I showed him the line that was drawn from the inset to one portion of the larger picture: the fly's eyeball. The inset was a close-up of the eye, its parts labeled. No caption explained what this was. The line from the eye to the inset was the only clue.

After explaining how I figured out the meaning of the inset, we turned to another page. Here was a praying mantis and another inset. I asked Elijah to figure out what this inset was showing us. No problem. Now that I had modeled for Elijah how I interpreted the connection between the large illustration and the inset, he understood that the inset on this page was a close-up of the mantis's leg.

Young readers need many experiences talking with an adult about the different pieces of information on a page and what it tells us. Sometimes there are informative text features in fiction, too—especially fiction for younger children—but in nonfiction, for adults and kids alike, there's a vast quantity of text features.

One of the most confusing of the text features is the article-within-an-article. Often these provide added information such as a short biography of the author, or one specific example of an event (such as one hurricane victim's story in an article on natural disasters, or a biography of a featured artist in an article that's mainly about the new local museum). An article-within-an-article may not be needed to understand the main text. In fact, children who stop in the middle of a text to read such an article (often embedded in the main text in a different-colored box) may get very confused.

Children don't always know that they are stopping one story to read another. They have to be taught that it's okay to skip these boxes and come back later, after they've understood the main text.

Number 4: Hearing the Text

Can you hear me now? CAN YOU HEAR ME NOW?!!! People who IM (instant message) each other do this all the time—writing in all caps and possibly with an excess of exclamation points in order to let the reader know that what they're seeing is louder and more intense than the rest of the text. You heard it, didn't you? Many young readers have to be taught this convention. It appears often in both fiction and nonfiction, not just in IMs. So do other forms of "heard" text.

Remember my buddy Elijah? Suppose he read this in his insect book: "Mrs. Black, a spider, is having a baby. She's pleased and proud. She invites her husband for a tender embrace. *Don't do it, Mr. Black.*"

Many children, unless explicitly taught, don't know that the italics signal a change in the tone of the text. As adult readers, we recognize a warning when we hear one. *But our kids can't hear it.* Not all of them, anyhow. If they don't hear it, they've missed the point. Something bad is about to happen to Mr. Black—something scary. His wife is about to become a widow—on purpose. A good reader uses textual clues to glean this information even before moving on to the next paragraph, where he may or may not be informed more explicitly. Sometimes the text will follow with an explanation. Sometimes not. Take this, for example:

> I knew that the killer was around somewhere, but Mrs. Grosvenor, at least, was safe. I knocked on her door. No answer. I knocked again. The door swung open. The room was empty and the window was open. *A length of knotted sheets was tied to the bedpost and tossed over the side of the window.*

We know that Mrs. Grosvenor shimmied down the sheets although the author never actually told us. We know that this is a dramatic and potentially deadly moment in the tale. Again, the author never told us any of this—not directly. We know all of this because we heard it through the change of tone signaled to us by the italics.

So simple, yet so complex. Would your child hear such important information in a story? Some more examples:

That's it. Did you hear it? When I wrote "Some more examples:" didn't you hear a pause right after the colon? Don't you know there's a change coming in the text—some more examples, perhaps, or maybe a list of some sort? Young readers won't hear such a pause unless you show them how you hear it.

Okay, for real now. Some more examples:

- Em dashes
- Parentheses
- Repetition

All of these signal a change in how the text is heard and understood. Em dashes—the long dashes that I am demonstrating in this sentence—let us hear an extra bit of information that is both part of a sentence and separate from it. (Needless to say, this is quite confusing for many young readers.)

And did you notice my use of the parentheses? It's almost like a Shakespearean play where a character says one thing and then turns aside and whispers something else. If our kids aren't taught to listen for changes signaled by these punctuation marks, a good deal of comprehension will be lost.

Repetition is important in poetry, in music, and sometimes in prose. Repetition adds intensity and is often a clue to the writer's main message. If you heard the following political speech, the repetition would signal the candidate's most important message.

My fellow Americans, my opponent, who has no military experience whatsoever, claims that we can win a war against Canada in six months. All it will take is a few hundred troops. Though he has no military experience, he says he has analyzed the situation and believes that Montreal can be taken in forty-eight hours. And what else has my opponent, who has no military experience, said? He said that Toronto can be taken in less than a day.

What's the message? His opponent is an idiot with no understanding of military tactics. The candidate never said this, but we know his point of view because he mentions over and over the fact that his opponent has no military experience.

Again, we need to clue our kids in to this strategy that writers use for getting across ideas. Don't leave it to chance. We have to teach our kids about repetition. We have to make them hear it or they will fail to comprehend the full import of what they're reading. Don't leave it to chance.

Number 5: Visualizing the Text

In the play *The Miracle Worker*, Annie Sullivan, Helen Keller's great teacher, is given these lines: "You think of her as a blind child. I ask that she see. I expect that she see." This is the goal of all adults who want to help youngsters become great readers. When reading fiction, our children literally have to see the text.

Skilled readers create pictures in their minds. You'd be surprised how many children don't. It's a sure sign that they don't fully comprehend what they're reading. And if they're not seeing the story, they're certainly not enjoying it.

To read fiction, you have to enter a world created by an author's imagination—but the author can't do it alone. The reader has to collaborate, to become the writer's coauthor. Consider these lines from *Alice's Adventures in Wonderland*:

> Either the well was very deep, or she fell very slowly, for she had plenty of time as she went down to look about her, and to wonder what was going to happen next. First, she tried to look down and make out what she was coming to, but it was too dark to see anything: then she looked at the sides of the well, and noticed that they were filled with cupboards and book-shelves: here and there she saw maps and pictures hung upon pegs. She took down a jar from one of the shelves as she passed: it was labeled "ORANGE MARMALADE," but to her great disappointment it was empty: she did not like to drop the jar, for fear of killing somebody underneath, so managed to put it into one of the cupboards as she fell past it.

What an amazing fantasy world Lewis Carroll has created for us; what a land of delight and indeed of wonder. But Carroll doesn't do it alone. Think of all the sights in this passage—the cupboards and shelves, the jar of marmalade, considerate Alice reaching for a shelf to replace the jar as she slowly floats downward. We take the words and flesh them out with our own mental images. No two readers see the same Wonderland. This book, like all works of fiction, is a collaboration between the author and each individual reader.

Many of our kids don't know this. They have to practice with you. If your child is reading a book, read it too. Pick out vivid passages and casually share with her what you see in your mind's eye.

"Wasn't it just crazy the way you think Alice is going to fall and hurt herself, and then she just floats down slowly like a feather? Do you think those cupboards are like the ones in our kitchen? I'm not sure; the book is so old that in my mind I see old-fashioned wood shelves, heavy ones, like in an old library. What do you see?"

You can practice this skill outside of books, too. Listen to the radio together, or books on tape. Discuss what you "see." Look at photographs and paintings and discuss what you envision just outside the image:

"Wow, this painting *The Scream* is really weird. What do you think the man in the picture is seeing?"

Or maybe:

"Look at this old photo of Grandma. There's a shadow on the grass next to her. Who do you think was standing just outside the camera's view?"

The more you stimulate a child's visual imagination, the more likely she'll be to apply it to her reading. Without a visual imagination, half of human intelligence would be lost to us.

Number 6: Summarizing

Summarizing is a very subtle form of visualizing. Teachers train students to summarize using various visual techniques. Young readers learn to "see" the important chunks of a story or nonfiction text. They also must be trained to see the connections among the parts.

This is often accomplished using visual devices—charts that teachers call *graphic organizers*. These are nothing more than diagrams that help readers organize facts and the relationships among facts in their heads. While reading, the child jots down brief notes (not whole sentences—*notes*) and uses the notes to retell what he learned. Don't turn it into a writing exercise. The notes should be jotted down quickly and used as a memory jogger. Sentence fragments are fine. We don't want to stop the flow of reading by having your child write a mini–*War and Peace*.

I'm only going to show you two graphic organizers because I don't want to overwhelm you. There are legions of them. These two are enough to help your child build comprehension. The first is called Intersecting Ovals. Note how the ovals overlap in the center. This one is used when figuring out how characters or events are both similar and different. The similarities are placed in the center while the qualities that are unique to each character, historical figure, place, or event are noted in the areas that don't intersect.

The figure shows a typical use of Intersecting Ovals. In a book about the ancient world, you might find a chapter on two ancient civilizations. There will be many facts. A strong reader will notice not just the facts but the thrust of the chapter—that the facts add up to a picture of two civilizations that were alike and different in their solutions to life's challenges.

If a young reader doesn't see this, then the disjointed facts will be largely meaningless to him. The Intersecting Ovals can help him focus on the big picture, which in this case is the relationship between the two civilizations. Help your child verbalize his notes and you are helping him summarize his reading. More than that, you're helping him to organize his thinking.

Now, I'm going backward. Most teachers will tell their students to look for causes and effects when summarizing events in a novel or nonfiction book. I have found that this causes confusion. Ask your child to do it the other way around. Start with the effect and then note the causes that led to that effect. Or to put it more simply: *What happened? What made it happen?* Here's a way to chart it out:

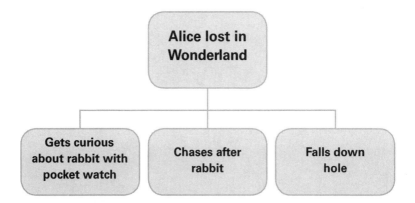

Your child can draw as many of the lower boxes as he needs, but if he overdoes it that's a clue that you need to guide him more closely in focusing on the important causes. The trick to using graphic organizers is to help your child use his mental butterfly net to capture the big ideas while letting the minor details flutter by without distracting him.

Now you know the Big Six. Work with your child on any one of these and her progress will amaze you. But knowing these skills is only part of the picture. Savvy parents also need to know how to choose the right books in which to practice these skills. In the next chapter, you will learn all about how to choose between books that are right for your child and books that aren't.

CHAPTER 2

Picking **Appropriate Books**

These days, there's a phrase you hear often at educational conferences. The phrase is *matching books to readers*. This involves determining a child's interests as well as providing her with books that are appropriately challenging—not too hard but just enough to build up the child's comprehension skills. When putting books in children's hands we must make sure that while the experience is educational it's not frustrating. Frustration will kill all our efforts to instill good reading habits and a love of reading. There are many aspects of matching books to readers but we must always remember that the most important thing is that young readers love the experience.

Assessing Your Child's Vocabulary

There's a common misconception about reading. Unfortunately, it's a misconception still popular in schools across the country. Give a child a challenging book and pressure her into reading it, and her literacy skills will improve. There's only one problem with this approach to literacy. It doesn't work.

Over the past ten years, I have attended scores of literacy conferences and I've heard the same message over and over. Books that are too hard do little to help children's skills improve. In fact, reading a very difficult book is so frustrating for many children that they become resistant readers.

Children who struggle at reading develop the conviction that reading makes no sense. The older they get, the more convinced they become that reading is a stressful activity to be avoided at all costs.

One response to this act of resistance is to lecture children on the importance of education. Frankly, it's a waste of time. Children are oriented to the here and now. They haven't yet developed the ability to set goals for a distant future—the future of adulthood and jobs. To lecture a child on preparing for the future, as many adults do, is an act of futility for adults and a cause of debilitating stress in children.

I won't bore you with the technical facts on how the brain works. I'll just give you the upshot. Stress shuts down the brain's learning center and fires up the self-defense portion of the brain. When learning becomes associated with stress, acquiring new knowledge and new skills becomes physically impossible. Much of the brain's energy is now focused on escaping unpleasantness.

Over countless generations, human beings have developed a unique survival skill. It's called pleasure. We find pleasure in food because that's the brain's way of telling us we must eat to survive. We find pleasure in sex because that's the brain's way of ensuring that our species will reproduce. The same is true for reading. If it's a pleasurable experience, it will be repeated. If reading provokes anxiety, we will avoid it the same way we avoid any unpleasant situation.

There's no way around it. If our children are to become avid and skilled readers, we must make it fun for them. This means that giving them books that are too hard will be counterproductive.

Determining a book's "rightness" is a little like Goldilocks' adventures in the home of the three bears. Was the porridge too hot, too cool, or just right? Is the book too hard, too easy, or just the right thing? How can we tell?

One way to tell is to use our fingers. When you're at the library or shopping in the bookstore, pull some books off the shelves. Randomly select a page in the middle of the book. Ask your child to read the page aloud and raise a finger every time she comes to a word she doesn't know. If there are only one or two unfamiliar words, she will probably be able to read the book on her own with minimal help.

If there are three to five unfamiliar words, she may struggle a bit. This is a book that you want to read together with your child, so she won't become frustrated. If you come across an unfamiliar word, just explain what it means and continue reading. Don't demand of your child that she look up every new word. This will diminish the flow of the story and reduce her enjoyment of the book. Also, dictionaries often provide definitions that include additional unfamiliar words. Using them can be daunting.

If there are more than five unfamiliar words, then the book will probably be too difficult for your child. It's better to wait until her vocabulary is larger. For ideas on how to increase your child's vocabulary, see Chapters 5 and 6.

The Feng Shui of Reading: Creating the Perfect Environment

The ancient Asian art of feng shui is used even today to create rooms and environments that are harmonious and relaxing. Everybody has his or her own idea of the perfect reading environment. You must remember, however, that your perfect environment may not be the same as your child's. Some people, for example, need dead silence; their concentration will waver if there's outside noise or music. Others find it easier to concentrate with their CD or iPod screwed into their ears. Others, like myself, can't read and listen to music at the same time, but read better when there's ambient noise.

The goal is to create an environment that works for your child. Begin by assessing your child's environmental likes and dislikes. Equally important is to teach your child to self-assess. Awareness of one's own preferred reading habits is a good step toward building lifelong literacy.

Additionally, by creating an optimal reading environment for your child, you're giving him a gift that schools can never provide. Schools, even newly built ones, largely follow a late-nineteenth-/early-twentieth-century assembly-line arrangement. Children sit in rows, spend a preset amount of time on a task, and then, at the prompting of a bell or whistle, move on to the next task. There might be some variations from school to school, but the model is largely the same.

Reading is limited in time and restricted by the environmental constraints set up by the school and the teacher. It is extremely unlikely that your child will find himself in a setting that is ideally suited to his reading needs. This is yet another reason why parents must support reading at home. Only you can ensure that your child will spend some quality reading time in an environment best suited to his personal reading habits.

The following checklist is designed to help you assess your child's habits. Give your child a book and allow him to arrange any space in the house the way he likes. Observe both where and how he reads.

Circle all that apply to your child.

Reading Environment Preference Checklist

My child prefers:

1. To read alone
2. To read in a hidden place (under the bed, in the attic, in the bathroom, etc.)
3. To read in a place where other people are constantly coming in and out
4. To stop and talk to others while reading
5. To ask questions or make comments while he reads
6. To remain uninterrupted
7. To read in a silent environment
8. To play the television while reading
9. To play music while reading
10. To talk on the phone while reading
11. To instant-message friends while reading

You will notice a pattern emerging. Your child is either a *solitary reader* or a *social reader*. Neither is better than the other. Both reading styles need monitoring. If your child is a social reader, for instance, periodically conduct some of the conversations outlined in Chapter 1. You want to make sure he's absorbing information and truly focusing. Don't assume he's not. Many people can chatter on the phone and read at the same time. Just make sure it's truly happening; otherwise his reading environment will have to be altered.

Social readers are easy to assess. They like talking about the books they're reading as adults are coming in and out of a room. Keep a few questions in mind as you pass by. When your child makes a comment about the book, seize the opportunity to ask an elaborating question. Be truly interested. Talk to your child; don't grill him.

"This book is weird, Mom."

"Really? I love weird books. Why is this one so strange?"

"The woman in the story is actually in love with the vampire."

"That is peculiar. Why do you think she chose him instead of a human being to love?"

If your child is a social reader, here are some environmental issues to keep in mind.

1. Don't stress him if he's watching TV while he's reading. Have him turn the TV off only if he's not really absorbing what he's reading.
2. Let him play music in his room if he wants to.
3. Try letting him read in a more "public" area such as the kitchen or the living room.
4. If he puts his feet up on the sofa or stretches out on the Oriental rug, let him. Your child's reading comfort is more important than your décor.
5. Let your child eat and read at the same time. Make sure, however, that if he's reading a library or school book his snack cannot cause stains. For library books, opt for pretzels rather than chocolate ice cream. Also keep an eye on how much he is eating as he reads. When distracted, it's easy to eat far more than is healthy.
6. Make sure that books are carried along on all family outings, from trips to the beach to your weekly excursions to the supermarket. If your child is very young, let him sit in the shopping cart with a favorite book. If he's older, don't stress him if he's walking and reading. Just keep an eye out and make sure that he doesn't collide with a stack of cans.
7. When visiting friends and relatives, don't torture your child by making him sit there silently with his hands folded. Let him bring a book and his iPod. If anyone has a question, he can

look up from his book, answer the question, and get back to reading.

8. Teach your child that reading isn't rudeness. Also, encourage the relatives you're visiting to ask about the book your child is reading.

Many children (and adults) fall into the category of *solitary reader*. These readers need a different sort of environment. Some of the needs are similar, but others are very different. Like social readers, solitary readers often like to sit on a rug or put their feet up on a piece of furniture. Let them. Again, within reason, let them snack while they're reading if they so choose. Solitary readers have needs that are sometimes harder to manage, especially if you have a large family. Here are some things to keep in mind.

1. Find a spot for your child that is completely private, or as isolated as possible.

2. If you have to buy a screen to partition off part of a shared bedroom or the living room, do so.

3. When your child is reading, keep noise to a minimum. If there is talking in the house or a TV playing, keep the sound as low as possible. If possible, have others in the house use headphones to listen to music or watch television.

4. Discuss the book with her after she's finished reading, not during. You can also discuss the book with her before she begins reading. Ask about where she left off or whether she's planning to read a certain number of pages or chapters. You can also ask her where she thinks the plot is going. Then afterward, ask if her guess was right or if she's changed her idea about the plot. "Actually, Dad, Tyrone can't be the person sending Mariah unsigned love notes. It turns out he's gay and he's in love with Anthony."

5. Resist the temptation to say "Go out and play." Some parents worry that their solitary readers will fail to make friends. This seldom happens, but they may not move in the same social circles as other children. When they want to read, let them read.

If reading is to become a lifelong habit, it must be pleasurable. That means that along with selecting books that your child enjoys, the reading environment must maximize the pleasantness of the experience. Many children become resistant readers because the only time they read is when they sit stiffly in an uncomfortable wood or plastic school chair in an environment where reading is a performance and not a joyful activity. In a world where test preparation parades as reading instruction we've turned a glorious pastime into drudgry. No wonder millions of kids are failing all over this country.

Assessing Your Child's Interests

Some parents take issue with the following statement, but your child's reading success depends on whether or not you accept this: Children have a right to their own taste. They have a right to read about subjects that interest them. You have an obligation to know your child's interests and to find books that grab him where he lives. Adults who try to force their notion of "good books" onto young readers will wind up with book-haters on their hands. Yes, I'm saying it. If your son likes Goosebumps or Cirque du Freak let him read the series. If your daughter likes the Babysitters Club, get her as many volumes as you can. If she prefers teen gossip mags, buy subscriptions and pile 'em high.

The most important and often the most overlooked element in raising strong readers is to develop reading stamina—the ability to stay with a book for extended periods of time. Think of it this way: Can you sit in a room with a relative or coworker who is totally boring and hang on their every word for an hour or more? Can you do this day in and day out for months or years? It's no different with reading. If the subject doesn't enthrall you and if the book isn't written in a style that captures your attention and carries you along, you won't be able to stay with it. Neither will your child.

So much of the national crisis in literacy is due to the fact that we try to force kids to read books that turn them off. And in school, they're often not reading books at all. They're reading test-prep passages. I would argue that many kids resist reading because they have good taste, and the literature being forced on them is as exciting as a spoonful of castor oil.

I'm not saying that your child should read *My Teacher Is an Alien* forever. But getting kids to read is a process. Today, video games, movies, and TV compete with books for our children's interest. Many of these large- and small-screen entertainments involve sci-fi fantasy elements, romance, and lots of action. These are the same things that our children want to read about.

Find those sorts of books and put them in your child's hands. Once he develops good reading habits, offer new books, new genres, and new themes. It's a matter of salesmanship. First, get him reading. Seduce him with topics that fascinate him. Once reading becomes a pleasurable habit, then offer a variety of new books. Try to expand your child's horizons by offering new, unexplored pleasures. Reading should always be an act of discovery.

The following interest inventory can help you determine which books might enchant your child. Circle any or all that apply to your child:

Interest Inventory

My child loves:

1. Cartoons and anime
2. Playing house
3. Anything to do with monsters and aliens
4. Dinosaurs
5. Things in nature (bugs, rocks, etc.)
6. Outer space
7. Animals
8. Sports
9. Superheroes
10. Famous people (actors and actresses, sports figures, etc.)
11. Poetry, rap, or hip-hop
12. Action-adventure stories
13. Science
14. Art
15. Making, preparing, or fixing things (model airplanes, sand-castles, recipes, clothing, etc.)

16. Mysteries
17. Romantic stories
18. Tough, urban tales
19. Mythology and folklore
20. The writing of a particular author

Now that you've inquired into your child's interests, the following guide will help you determine the genres that correspond to the topics he or she likes.

If your child likes cartoons and anime, he or she will love graphic novels. These generally fall into the categories of action adventure, sci-fi fantasy, horror, and historical fiction.

If your child loves to play house, take a look at nonfiction books and magazines on cooking and home decorating. Cook simple recipes together while teaching your child how to interpret the directions. Gradually move your child toward more and more independence while still keeping an eye on the proceedings. Safety always comes first.

If your child loves anything to do with monsters and aliens, go to the sci-fi shelves. There are both chapter books and graphic novels in this category.

If your child loves dinosaurs, it's time for a trip to your local natural history museum. Museums often sell books on a variety of scientific topics. Dinosaurs are popular, so you'll likely find books about them in the children's section. Older children will be able to select from the adult section.

If your child loves things in nature see your local museum for books on science and natural history. Science and natural history books are great for reading together, even with teens. Collect samples (if you can tolerate captured insects in your home) and look at the various illustrations and captions and try to identify different parts. Alternately, go on field trips with your child and help find and examine the bugs, rocks, etc., that interest him or her.

If your child loves outer space, there are plenty of books on this subject for all ages. Also, rent videos on the topic and discuss them together. This will build up your child's knowledge of science. It's also a great vocabulary-building activity. Children who love outer space will likely take to both science books and sci-fi. One fun critical-thinking activity is to discuss whether the events in a sci-fi novel could really happen. Some sci-fi books are pure fantasy. Others base their plots on popular scientific speculation.

If your child loves animals, you'll have no trouble finding books about them. There are loads of nonfiction books about animals as well as action adventure novels that involve animals. Younger children love picture books in which animals are the protagonists. There's an endless supply of those, as well as chapter books for very young readers.

If your child loves sports, look for action-adventure books and biographies of famous sports figures. If you go to a sporting event, teach your child how to read and interpret the scores. This activity will build a child's reading and math skills at the same time.

If your child loves superheroes, you'll find plenty of graphic novels and comic books. Yes, comic books. These are great vocabulary builders. Also, you can teach your child interpretive skills by discussing the connection between the images and the words in a comic book. Make sure you examine the bubbles together so that your child learns to distinguish between thought bubbles (the ones that look like clouds) and speech bubbles (the ones with arrows pointing toward a character's mouth). A child's failure to distinguish between thought bubbles and speech bubbles interferes with his or her comprehension.

If your child loves famous people (actors and actresses, sports figures, etc.), look for the myriad biographies and autobiographies that are available for children of all ages. Don't turn your nose up at magazines, either. If your children are reading gossip magazines and sports magazines, then they're *reading*. That's the goal, isn't it? And these magazines present powerful opportunities to develop your child's moral decision-making skills. You can discuss why an actress became anorexic or a sports figure took steroids. Often it's hard for parents to bring up difficult topics. But if they come up naturally as part of a discussion about a magazine article, you have the opportunity to provide moral guidance in an easy-to-introduce manner. Certainly, this is a time to introduce your own beliefs, but it's also a time to ask your child to discuss how he or she would handle—or avoid—such situations.

If your child loves poetry, rap, or hip-hop, listen to music together and discuss the lyrics. Here's where you have some personal decisions to make. Many lyrics contain strong language. Some parents prefer to expose their children to such words and discuss the rightness and wrongness of certain choices. Others insist that children should not be exposed to such language at all. Neither decision is better or worse. The only bad decision is to allow your child to be exposed to strong language without discussing your take on such words. Also, I urge you to listen to rap, hip-hop, and rock lyrics before your child is exposed to them. Often, the words on an album are much stronger than the version broadcast on the radio. So, *buyer beware!*

If your child loves action-adventure stories, there are plenty for children of all ages. These can come in the form of fantasy stories, outdoor-adventure stories, sports stories, mysteries, spy novels, and animal adventures. Action-adventure is a great way to expand your child's horizons. If, for example, your child loves science fiction, you might want to offer some mysteries or spy novels. Often one interest leads to the next. Reading a variety of genres builds vocabulary and a broader familiarity with the world—what experts call *background knowledge*.

If your child loves science, museums and hobby shops often sell kits that enable you to do experiments together. Following directions is a big part of reading. You're also building more of the background knowledge that will help your child become a smart reader.

If your child loves art, there are two ways to go. There are "how-to" books that teach children how to paint, draw, take photographs, etc. Again, this is a great way for children to learn how to follow directions. Books that contain reproductions of famous art works build background knowledge. Many of these books tell about the lives and times of the artists. Readers come away knowing much about the world.

If your child loves making, preparing, or fixing things (model airplanes, sandcastles, recipes, clothing, etc.), then get kits and teach your child to build, cook, sew, etc. This is a great way to develop practical life skills. If your child is willing to do these activities with you, then you've gone a long way toward building a lifetime of loving memories.

If your child loves mysteries, you can find them for every age. Even *Where's Waldo?* is a type of mystery. Looking for clues, making predictions, and assessing the accuracy or inaccuracy of one's predictions are all forms of critical thinking. Mysteries go a long way toward developing the brain's reasoning skills.

If your child loves romantic stories, there are plenty of these books on the market. The field is especially rich for readers in their teens or early adolescence. Fairy tales often contain romantic elements as well. These days, there are even romance novels for youngsters and some adult romance novels tend more toward the romantic than the racy—though as a parent you'd have to be willing to risk your child being exposed to some adult language and themes. That's your judgment call, parents.

If your child loves tough, urban tales, you'll have great opportunities to discuss moral issues. There are urban tales and problem novels that deal with very serious life issues. You can even find picture books that deal with life's complex problems. Make sure you read these books before giving them to your child. Decide whether your child is ready to handle such books. Make sure *you* are ready to handle such books, too. Try to anticipate questions that your child might ask and be prepared with answers that you think he or she can handle. Teens often find it hard to talk to adults about painful issues. Discussions about problem novels or urban fiction might give them an opportunity to open up to you.

If your child loves mythology and folklore, help extend this into cultural awareness. Tales from around the world are available in our libraries and bookstores. These tales of mythology and folklore achieve two goals. First, they build pride in one's own culture, which is especially important for communities that have been marginalized throughout history. Pride is the first step toward achievement. Second, they build awareness of other cultures. In our increasingly global economy, respect for other cultures is not only desirable, it's an economic survival skill. Knowledge of mythology and folklore will also improve reading comprehension later in life because so many novels are built upon themes and characters to be found in world mythology. Authors often take for granted that the reader understands the cultural references in their novels. The reader who lacks awareness of such references can misinterpret the book.

If your child loves the writing of a particular author, get as many books by this author as possible. Build critical thinking by discussing themes that repeat in the author's work. If the author writes a series about the same characters, discuss whether the characters change or behave similarly across the series. If possible, read the series in order because there are often references in the later novels that will make no sense unless you've read the earlier books.

You have just begun a great family adventure. You and your child can discuss any of the genres on the list that interest her. You can find many books on each of these topics. Here are some possible ways to find them.

1. **Ask your child's teacher.** If you're lucky, he'll have a classroom library with some of these genres. If not, ask for recommendations of authors and titles.
2. **Ask your librarian.** Certainly there will be books on the shelves. Your librarian can probably order additional books in a series or provide catalogues of topics from which she can order new books—if her budget allows. Interlibrary loan services might also be accessed. If a desired book is in another library in your city, very often it can be shipped to your local branch.
3. **Look in bookstores.** If you can afford the books, great. If not, jot down the titles you want and go back to the library to order them for free. (Mr. Barnes and Mr. Noble are probably turning over in their graves, but what the heck. It's our kids and we'll get them books any way we can within the limits of the law.) Don't forget, you can look online at Amazon and Barnes & Noble, where used books can be had VERY cheaply. Once you look at one book, these Web sites will offer many additional titles ("People who ordered xxx also ordered yyy").
4. **Talk to other parents.** Ask them what their kids like.
5. **Ask your child's friends what they like.** A recommendation from another child can be powerful inducement to read a book.

Never forget the power of the Internet. Search on Google for some of the following phrases (and think of some of your own) and you will come up with a nearly endless universe of databases.

1. Children's literature
2. Children's books
3. Award-winning children's books
4. Young adult literature
5. Popular books for teens

6. Fiction for children
7. Nonfiction for children
8. Books for young readers
9. Children's picture books
10. Children's chapter books

Don't forget to do a Google search for your child's favorite authors. These days, most of them have their own Web sites with lists of books and even the titles of upcoming books. Often these authors have links to other pages that might interest your child. If your child is old enough, teach him how to search the Internet for topics of interest. If your child is learning how to negotiate the features of a Web site or database, this is reading instruction, too. For more on this topic, see Chapter 3.

A Note on Fantasy

Without a doubt, the Harry Potter books are the most popular children's series in history. They are also among the most controversial. The books have been condemned from pulpits across the country. Many people revile the books because the characters are wizards. The books teach witchcraft, is the oft-heard complaint.

Series such as the Harry Potter books, Garth Nix's Old Kingdom trilogy (including *Sabriel*, a personal favorite, recommended to me by a highly literate twelve-year-old), and John Christopher's Tripod novels serve an important function. These books fall squarely within the tradition of ancient mythology and Gothic literature.

They are tales of good versus evil. The protagonists are undeterred in their fight against the villains even if those villains are terrifying. Villains may be daunting, but the heroes and heroines of these stories work up the nerve to carry on. These books can inspire the reader, since they help her to get past her own fear, muster real courage, and meet difficult challenges. People have been writing such tales since the dawn of literacy. It is more than a little shortsighted to condemn fantasy literature.

When children read such books, they put themselves in the place of the heroes. They imagine themselves combating evil and winning. I've never met a child who fantasizes about being the *loser*. Putting oneself in the shoes of a fantasy hero is a natural way for children to imagine themselves changing the world for the better. Later in life, such children may become explorers, scientists, politicians, educators, religious leaders—and often these goals began in the world of the imagination.

To deny a child the opportunity to imagine himself as a hero is to deny early moral growth. Few children believe these stories in the literal sense. Children aren't as fragile as we sometimes believe. They won't have their sense of reality warped by Harry Potter or by *The Princess and the Goblin*. Children live in the world of possibility, not in the world of psychosis, except for the rare few who are truly disturbed.

Adults often distinguish between fantasy and "serious" books. This is a mistake. What could be more serious than the battle between good and evil? And what can be more powerful than the imagination? Yesterday's fantasy is today's reality. Jules Verne wrote about submarines before they existed. H. G. Wells wrote about space travel when the notion was pure fantasy.

Fantasy and sci-fi allow children to stretch their imaginations in all sorts of unexpected directions. This broadens the mind. Today's fantasy reader may grow up to be a creative problem solver, a person who solves life's problems in new and imaginative ways. If we force children to stick with our notions of what is real, we may be retarding their future abilities to find original solutions to long-standing problems.

Our Youngest Readers

There are many books for emerging readers, those who are just learning the conventions of print. There's a problem with many of these books. They're written for contemporary adults rather than for children. They're designed for the purchaser, a grownup with a taste for striking graphics and text that appears in a variety of visually interesting places on the page. This type of book, while lovely to look at, is problematic for emerging readers.

Many new readers need regularity in order to begin learning the conventions of printed literature. The best books for emerging readers have short, simple sentences on the top or bottom of the page.

Each sentence should begin and end on one page. Later, when your child is more sophisticated, she can begin to learn that sentences roll from one page to the next.

Books for emerging readers should contain illustrations that clearly link up the printed words with the events in the story. The more a child can link the pictures with the words, the faster her vocabulary will grow.

"And who is that?"

"It's Poppa Bear."

"What is he doing with his lips?"

"He's blowing on the porridge because it's too hot."

"And what's this word I'm pointing to?"

"Hot!"

When reading aloud to an emerging reader, always point to the pictures and ask your child what's going on in the illustration. Also, as you're reading the text, point to each word with your finger so your child can see and hear the word at the same time. Many readers struggle when they can't make the connection between the sound and sight of a word, so make sure your child makes the connection.

If your child picks up the connection between words and images quickly, then you can move on to more sophisticated picture books. There are lots of books that have interesting themes and images, but before you expose her to those, make sure she doesn't get confused by complicated graphics.

CHAPTER 3

Modern Literacies: From **Web Sites** to **Video Games**

There are many new contemporary forms of reading. Children are quite good at some of these but poor at others. One of the weaker areas is Internet research. Secondary schools especially often claim they are preparing their students to do research on the Web when in fact they're doing nothing of the kind.

School research projects often include the use of online research. However, many teachers focus on the content of their subject areas but do little or nothing to teach the ins and outs of Internet research. A typical research project assignment might look something like this:

Ms. Chilblain
American History I
Directions: Identify the causes of the Civil War. In your project be sure to include:

- The important events leading up to the Civil War
- The important people who helped cause the war
- The major events that occurred while the war was raging.

Be sure to include at least five sources in your report. These can include encyclopedias, biographies, history books, and Web sites.
Length: 5 pages
Due date: October 24

At the start of such a project, many teachers will take their class to the school's library/media center. The librarian will give a short talk on the different sources of information available and then the students will be told to get to it. If the students are really lucky, they'll also have a school computer lab where they can do their research without competing for time on the computers. If they're really, *really* lucky they'll be given the names of a few relevant Web sites.

So what's missing? A lot! Learning is not only a *what* but a *how*. Students must, at every age, learn the process of gathering information as well as the content of each subject. Modern literacies—and Web sites are among these—have a great variety of features that one must know and use.

Think back to Chapter 1, where you learned about text features. Savvy readers know how these features work in books. They also know how to use the text features on Web sites. Extremely savvy readers know that there's a *connection* between the text features in books, on graphs and maps, and on Web sites. Teachers rarely teach these connections. So, parents, once again it's up to you to do it.

The typical nonfiction book, for example, has a table of contents. A map has a key (sometimes called a legend). So do many charts. And Web sites? They help readers locate information in various ways. Among the most common are informational keys (yes, Web sites have them too), pull-down menus, highlighting, and icons (little pictures).

Informational Keys

These can usually be found across the top or along the left-hand side of a Web site. A reader must decide what information they're looking for and make a judgment about which item on the key is most likely to lead them to it.

This isn't all that different from using a table of contents. The table might lead you to a particular chapter. The chapter then is subdivided and labeled by headings. There might also be illustrations (like the one you just looked at), sidebars, and captions.

All of this can be daunting for children. We can help them by explicitly teaching them how informational keys work. Talk through several Web pages with your child. Verbalize your decision-making process as you search for information.

> I think I'll click on the General Parenting button because I think, since it's called "general" parenting, there'll be books on lots of interesting topics for a parent like me.

After you've done this for your child on several occasions, give her the opportunity to verbalize her thinking process in the same way that you modeled your own. Don't worry if she doesn't get it right the first time. This is a complicated process and many children need time to get it right. The more modeling you do, and the more you and your child verbalize your thinking, the more successful she will be.

Let's look at Ms. Chilblain's assignment again. There's another problem with it. Essentially, it's an invitation to plagiarize. This often happens when students do Internet research. They find the information asked for and copy it verbatim (only adding in a few of their own words, perhaps). Sometimes, students just print out the article and hand it in exactly as it is.

If Ms. Chilblain were to see such a thing, she would give the paper an automatic zero. The student would be angry, thinking herself abused. After all, she did the report, didn't she? In a way the answer is yes. She located and handed in the information required. What difference would it make if a student uses the Web author's words or her own? "Besides," I've often heard kids say, "I don't know how to put it in my own words."

The entire situation could have been avoided if Ms. Chilblain had asked more sophisticated questions. Think back to Chapter 1, where I presented a series of in-depth conversations you and your child can have about literary characters. The same types of thinking can be encouraged during report writing.

Children must be encouraged to do original thinking, not just to spit back facts. When they do this thinking, their writing will come out in their own words. When creativity is required, no Web site or encyclopedia can provide exact answers to be copied. Originality will therefore come naturally.

Obviously, you can't make Ms. Chilblain change her assignment, but many parents review their children's assignments. You can follow up by asking in-depth questions of your own. This might not change anything with Ms. Chilblain, but your child will be moved to a deeper level of thinking. The benefits of such thinking are both long-term and priceless.

Consider this:

Dr. Lanse
American History I
Topic: The Civil War
In your project be sure to:

- Explain what the outbreak of the war teaches us about human nature. Were the people of the North and South good, evil, or a combination of both? Explain your reasons. Make sure your explanation includes a discussion of at least three historical figures of the time.
- Compare the American Civil War to any other war you learned about. How were the causes similar and different?
- Explain whether you think the war was a good thing or a bad thing if you were a:
  - White Southerner
  - Black Southerner
  - White Northerner

Additionally, list the sources you use and explain how you found these sources. You must use at least five different sources of information.

Notice how this assignment requires a deeper level of thinking than Ms. Chilblain's? There's no reason why you can't have conversations like this even if the teacher doesn't require it.

Even better, if you're an activist parent (my favorite kind) and you become a member of your local school board or leadership team, you can advocate for deeper training so that Ms. Chilblain and others like her can teach at a higher level. It's a goal worthy of pursuing if you can, but remember: Don't leave it all up to the schools. Your child needs you *now*.

Pull-Down Menus

Modern literacies actually require that the reader possess a greater combination of skills than traditional books. Your child will need to manipulate moving, changing images in order to retrieve information. A pull-down menu is a variation on the informational key. The problem with pull-downs is that their presence isn't always obvious.

Children need to know that when they first encounter a Web site they've got to play across the images with the cursor to test for pull-down menus. Other modern literacies provide not a pull-down but a scroll-down menu.

Highlighting

Highlighting or color-coding is another way to locate information. Highlighting is not exclusive to modern literacy, but it's a very big part of it. Children need to be taught to look for highlighting in many different places.

When very young, most children learn that the color red means *stop*, be it in a traffic light or on a stop sign. In elementary school social studies lessons, they may learn some of the rudiments of map skills. Blue means *water*; green means *land*. On the secondary level, students might learn a few more bits of information about color-coding on maps and charts. Rarely do they learn that colored highlights on Web sites are also meant to alert them to important information.

On maps, for example, blue means water. On Web sites, it can mean something very different. Blue means *this is a link*. If a Web address is given in blue, children must learn that all they need to do is click the words highlighted in blue to get to that link. Does your child know this? How can they unless you've demonstrated?

Often, a Web site will highlight new vocabulary words in blue. Again, this is a link. Click the word and you will get to the definition or another article. Savvy readers know that this is similar to looking up words in a glossary or reading a sidebar.

Having all this information can be a blessing or a comprehension challenge, depending on the skill level of the particular reader. Many young readers get confused if they click on every link as they read. They lose the flow of the main article. They must be taught that reading printed nonfiction articles and Web articles must be done more than once.

This again is where modeling comes in. Show your child how you read through most of the article once, to get the main information. Then you go back and read the links to get additional information. The only time you stop and use a link the first time around is when a vocabulary word impedes your understanding so much that the rest of the article can't be understood.

Model for your child how you ask yourself, "Do I mostly understand what's going on in this article? If so, I'll keep reading. If I don't, I'm going to stop and check my understanding of the new vocabulary in the article." Good readers are forever making considered choices about whether to pause or to keep reading. Readers who don't make such conscious choices often wind up lost and confused.

Young readers must also be taught that colors other than blue often represent links within a Web site. Demonstrate how you play the cursor across a Web page and how changes in color when you do so indicate the presence of a link. This is another form of informational key. Again, young readers must have an adult demonstrate how they decide which link to click once they see where the highlighted links are located.

Icons

Icons have long been used as informational symbols. Go to any restaurant in any country and you can tell the difference between the men's room and women's room just by looking at the symbols on the door. You don't have to know the language. When crossing the street, if the little walking man lights up, it's time to move. You don't need to see the word *walk*. Modern literacies rely heavily on such icons. Children need practice interpreting symbols in order to effectively use the Internet, cell phones, video games, and so on.

Of course, it will help if they understand that visual images similar to the more contemporary icons are used in more traditional texts as well. Look in any social studies book. There will be plenty of maps. Many maps use icons. A series of upside down Vs, for example, represent a mountain range. Mapmakers often think of a symbol of this sort as "obvious," so they may not provide an explanation of the symbol. However, many children don't understand such symbols automatically. They must be explicitly taught what a symbol means.

Other maps indicate the meaning of symbols on their map keys. Adults must model for children how they use the key to interpret the symbols. You have probably seen maps with little ears of corn, for example. These represent an agricultural region. Little wheelbarrows with black spots inside representing lumps of coal may indicate an industrial region. Little stick figures may represent the size of the population in a given locale. The more stick figures, the denser the population. We cannot assume that children will understand these things if we don't teach them.

Building comprehension of icons can go two ways. You can begin by teaching your child the meaning of particular icons. Later, encourage him to create his own icons. This is a simple, fun, and highly educational process. Your child can draw pictures that symbolize different rooms in the house. Then post those symbols in front of those rooms. If your child doesn't like to draw, cut pictures out of magazines. For further ideas, see Chapter 9 on the reading/writing connection.

IM Lingo

Along with icons, there's another aspect of modern literacy that every parent should know: online shorthand, which is often used in instant messages (IMs). Online shorthand is quickly learned by many children because it provides them with a secret language. It's important to know these terms in order to protect your child from online predators. If you see a 9 (parent is watching) or PBB (parent behind back), you'll want to find out what's going on immediately. Use an Internet search engine such as Google to search for "IM lingo for parents" (or a similar phrase) to familiarize yourself with this secret language your child is most likely using.

There's another reason to concern yourself with online shorthand. It influences your child's writing. Many children get poor grades on writing assignments because they substitute shorthand for words.

Many children can't distinguish between the two. Teachers frequently penalize their students for using such shorthand, but they rarely provide lessons on translating shorthand into conventional words.

You can help at home. Write messages to your child using shorthand. Ask your child to rewrite your messages in standard English. Make a game of it. Teachers too often approach this issue punitively. Online shorthand is a new writing system, part of your child's world and part of the world of many adults. It has a legitimate place in our lives. Children need to understand, however, that shorthand has its place and so does conventional English.

Video Games

One of the most controversial of the modern literacies is video games. They're often viewed as mindless, violent entertainment. But the research on video games presents a more complex picture. Video games:

- Improve one's ability to interpret icons
- Improve visual/spatial reasoning
- Train children to respond quickly to multiple visual images
- Train children to comprehend multiple, intersecting narratives
- Train children to infer rules that are not directly stated
- Encourage children to test their skills in a relatively low-risk environment
- Improve social skills

Whether we like it or not, our society has become increasingly visually oriented. This doesn't mean that there's less pressure on children to become good readers. The intellectual demands on children are greater than at any other time in history. In order to function in the working world, our children will have to interpret print literature and a vast visual language.

Think of television. Those of you who are baby boomers, think back to the 1960s. TV shows had simple plot lines. Today, most shows have multiple intersecting plot lines, flashbacks, even internal fantasy sequences. The average TV viewer must interpret all of these elements and understand the connections among them.

Video games are even more complex. Your child will not only have to interpret intersecting plot lines, he'll have to choose which plot lines to follow. Many video games are interactive, allowing the gamer to choose the plot direction or the movements of characters. This provides great interpretive challenges. In order to succeed, one must make good decisions—and quickly.

As soon as one makes choices, there are new stimuli to respond to—perhaps an attacking alien or a seductive secret agent. In order to improve at a game, one must respond quickly to such stimuli, which are the results of one's choices. Additionally, the gamer must move from one platform to the next. This means that he must learn from his mistakes and make new, better, faster choices with each new game.

To a very large extent, our children *do* succeed. And this is important. If we mistakenly view these successes as nothing more than good gaming we'll miss the fact that the speed and accuracy of our children's intellectual abilities has grown. Many contemporary, technology-based industries require skilled workers who can make quick and accurate decisions. And can you imagine a banker, a military leader, or a schoolteacher succeeding without the ability to respond quickly to changing circumstances? The skills needed to be a successful gamer can be applied in many industries. If your child is a gamer, applaud his successes the same way that you would applaud a good report card. Both successes are equally as valid.

When it comes to the rules of video games, your child may have one of two challenges. Earlier, you read about building reading stamina (stick-to-it-iveness) when it comes to reading a text. Stamina is required when reading the rules of many games. Some of these rules run the length of a small book. Some children will give up. If your child has practiced reading lots of books in a comfortable reading environment, then it's likely he'll stick with reading the rules. If he hasn't spent his childhood building stamina, then reading gaming rules (or a VCR manual or microwave instructions or a recipe) will be frustrating.

Some games provide another challenge. The rules can only be inferred while playing the game. This means that in order to win, one must figure out what's going on. Can you imagine waking up on an island filled with people, all of whom are having complex interactions with each other and with you—and you don't even know the purpose for the gathering? What if your livelihood, or even your life, depended on figuring out the social rules in this odd and ominous environment? This may sound bizarre, but such imaginative games have their application to real-world circumstances. Research tells us that job success often depends on a person's ability to "read" rapidly changing social rules, especially the unwritten ones that can only be inferred while interacting with others.

If your kid's a gamer, he's doing it all the time, conceptually at least. What one can do conceptually can, in time, be applied to situations in real life. So have a little respect. And *express* that respect. Be proud. Your approval is a great motivating factor in your child's life and one of the simplest routes to success of any kind.

One of the best ways to encourage your child's critical thinking while gaming is to play with him. Don't pressure him to attain a particular level. Just have fun and keep trying to top yourselves—not each other. The nature of these games is such that your child's skills will develop naturally.

If you're not prepared to play, at least watch. Many children love to verbalize what they're doing as they're playing. In Chapter 1, you learned the importance of talk when analyzing characters. Talk is just as important in figuring out how to be a successful gamer. Talking will help your young gamer think through his strategies and beef up his intellectual prowess. And of course, these conversations will bring you and your child closer, which is always a benefit.

Because of their dramatic content, video games are highly controversial. There continues to be much debate on violence in video games. Some experts are convinced that violent video games, because of their interactive nature, are more dangerous than violent movies or TV programs. Others claim that children who turn violent after playing such games are already disturbed and would not have reacted so if they didn't already have severe psychological problems.

Others would argue that violent entertainment has always been a part of culture. Didn't Oedipus gouge out his eyes? Didn't Romeo and Juliet commit double-suicide? Aren't contact sports inherently violent?

Whether we like it or not, violent entertainment is with us. Videos are part of that fare. The decision regarding whether or not to allow your children to play these games is your own. However, if you do decide to allow them to be exposed to these violent video games, it is imperative that you monitor the impact of video games on your child. Then, you can decide whether or not you should allow your child to continue playing.

CHAPTER 4

Meditation for a Better Brain

This chapter is for your child and for you. Stress reduces the brain's ability to absorb and retain information. A stressed-out child is a child who cannot live up to her full intellectual potential. A stressed-out parent creates a stressed-out home environment. So anything that can relieve stress will improve a child's ability to read well and think well.

One of the great stress reducers is meditation. Before you say to yourself, "Meditation is not my thing," think about this: Meditation has incredible physiological and psychological benefits. Meditation can:

- Improve concentration
- Relieve anxiety
- Boost your resistance to clinical depression
- Boost your immune system
- Lower your blood pressure
- Reduce the risk of heart disease
- Help you manage pain such as backaches and headaches
- Help you or your child handle anger and frustration
- Create an overall sense of well-being and bliss

Meditation is great at any age, but it can be especially helpful to teens who are trying to weather the storms of adolescence. At any age, reducing stress allows the intellect to function more freely. This chapter will cover a variety of meditation and stress-reducing techniques that will help relieve both your and your child's stress. Among these are:

- Mindfulness meditation
- Mantra meditation
- Physical meditation
- Guided imaging

Meditation and the Brain

Following is a brief description of the impact of meditation on the brain. In recent years, scientific studies have begun to show that meditation literally changes the physical composition of the human brain. The cerebral cortex (the thin, outer layer of brain cells) grows denser with new cell growth.

The structures that grow thicker are those that regulate our attention span and our working memory (our ability to hold several bits of information in our minds at once as we puzzle out a problem). In other words, regular meditation can make us more focused and *smarter*!

Let me throw another biological term your way—the *cingulate gyrus*. It's the portion of your brain associated with learning. Those who meditate enrich the cingulate gyrus with greater blood flow than normal. This, plus an alteration in the brain's electrical impulses, seems to improve brain functioning. Cool, huh?

Okay, enough of the biology lesson. The upshot is: If you and your child meditate together, the benefits will be manifold. Meditation is brain therapy. Meditation is a path to greater learning and critical-thinking skills. It will certainly help your child with reading stamina and with learning in general. Importantly, meditation will reduce the stressors that impede learning.

Following are descriptions of various types of meditation and stress-reducing techniques. Different techniques work for different people, so if one doesn't work for you or your child, try some of the others. A word of caution: Don't give up too quickly. Give each method six to eight weeks before giving up on it. It takes a while to develop and maintain a meditation practice. Children, who are often more impulsive than adults, may take longer. Stick with it.

Mindfulness Meditation

This is the form of meditation often referred to when people talk about Zen. Sometimes you'll hear phrases like "being in the moment" or "being at one" with an object. Mindfulness meditation has also been referred to as "one-pointed" meditation. All of this simply means that the mind has developed the ability to maintain a laserlike focus on a single object of contemplation.

The bad news is that it takes lots of time (years for some people) to develop this ability. The good news is that even a partial mastery of this technique provides life-altering benefits. Think of all the times you've read twenty pages of a book only to realize that you have no idea what you just read. Think of all the conversations you've had where it suddenly dawns on you that you haven't listened to a word for the past ten minutes.

Now imagine what life would be like if these concentration problems diminished. Imagine how much more successful your child would be in school if her mind didn't wander. These are the benefits of mindfulness meditation.

Always begin mindfulness meditation by sitting in a comfortable position. You don't have to bend yourself like a pretzel and sit in the classic lotus position. Any comfortable chair will do fine. The only thing you don't want to do is lie down. This increases the likelihood that you'll doze off. Meditation is not the same as napping. The brain functions differently when you fall asleep.

Make sure that you and your child are wearing loose, comfortable clothing and that the room is neither too warm nor cold. Now let's look at some examples of mindfulness meditation. Learn them for yourself first; then you can try them with your child.

The Breath

Perhaps the most common object of mindfulness is the breath. Just sit and breathe for a moment. Focus your mind on the act of breathing in and out. Where does your attention settle? In your abdomen? In your chest? At your nostrils? Wherever you naturally focus is the area that becomes your center of mindfulness.

Follow your breathing. Try to banish all words and thoughts from your mind. If you're trying it, right about now you might be getting very frustrated. Many people, in the beginning, can't go for more than ten seconds without feeling their minds invaded by their own thoughts. There's a constant stream of inner noise. Some call it "chatter"; the ancient Buddhists called it "monkey mind."

When you experience monkey mind, the next thought is "This isn't going to work. I can't meditate." The answer to that is: You already are meditating. Through meditation, you've just become aware of the inner workings of your own mind. You've always had the chatter, but it's so much a part of you that it's always been in the background of your consciousness.

Now the noise is front and center. Becoming aware of it is part of the meditation process. Uncomfortable, isn't it? But here's the thing: Those who are aware of their thoughts have more control over them. If you have a lot of angry thoughts, for example, and you know it, you have reduced the likelihood of an angry and compromising outburst at work. Your child, if aware of her thoughts, is less likely to express anger in a way that will get her in trouble at school.

Slowly, over time, as you get better at sustaining focus on your breath, you will have fewer angry (or depressed or anxious) thoughts because you'll get better at concentrating on your breath. As a result, you'll feel more comfortable under your own skin. So too will your child.

Mandalas

One traditional object of mindfulness is the mandala. A mandala is a circular object of contemplation on which to focus the mind. Mandalas often have intersecting spirals that have a hypnotic effect on the viewer. The longer you stare at them, the more they draw you into the center.

For some people, these objects make it easier to keep the chattering voices out of their heads and to develop that one-pointed concentration I spoke of earlier. You literally are focusing on one point. The intersecting spirals of a mandala can create the illusion of movement. The viewer experiences a spinning or spiraling sensation. For some this can be mesmerizing. For others it can be dizzying.

If you or your child experiences discomfort when contemplating a mandala, then drop it and try another technique. If it works for you and your child, great! Part of the meditation process is the search for techniques that work for you. Treat the whole thing as an adventure.

You and your child can also treat it as a game. Search for mandalas on the Internet and print out those that you and your child like. Talk about which colors you both find attractive. Another alternative is to make your own. Put together images with glued construction paper, washable paint, or crayons. If you have access to one of those old-fashioned spin-art machines, the paintings you can create with these make ideal mandalas. A compass and colored pencils will also yield do-it-yourself mandalas.

If mandalas are not your thing, you have other visual choices: a favorite painting, the landscape outside your window, a favorite figurine. Buddhists often contemplate statues or busts of the Buddha, but you don't have to practice Eastern religions to meditate. You may even try a favorite doll or action figure. The point is to relax and to focus your attention at the same time. Any object of contemplation can do the trick.

Mantra Meditation

Mantra meditation is a form of mindfulness in which a short sound, phrase, prayer, or affirmation is repeated over and over. One of the most famous is "OM." The ancients had all sorts of explanations for the meanings of such sounds. You don't have to buy into any belief system, however, in order to do mantra meditation.

Many people find that the repetition of a sound and the concentration on one's own voice help to banish the chattering within. Mantras have an added dimension. They can help the meditator focus on specific goals or values.

If you select a specific prayer, whatever your religion, your consciousness centers around the spiritual values embedded in that prayer. If you choose an affirmation, you can repeatedly remind yourself of a specific life goal or value that you're trying to embrace.

You and your child can develop affirmations of your own, but here are a few you may want to try together. Don't select an affirmation on your own. Choose one or more with your child. Discuss the meaning of the affirmation and talk about why your child thinks it's a good choice. Notice that these affirmations deal with much more than just reading and learning. They can be used to help your child (and you) move closer to many important life goals.

School Affirmations

These can help your child focus on positive school goals and can help build self-esteem.

- I can focus on my book; I can stay with my book.
- I find joy in reading; I find joy in books.
- Knowledge is power; learning is my strength.
- My mind is clear; my thoughts are wise.
- There is no fear in learning; the whole world is an open book.

Emotional-Control Affirmations

These will help your child master emotional states that interfere with learning and social relationships.

- Breathing in, my anger cools; breathing out it vanishes like smoke.
- Out goes anger; in comes love.
- I release my worries; I release my fears.
- I am quiet inside; I am peaceful inside.
- I'm a flower blowing in the breeze; I'm a cloud floating in the sky.

Sport and Performance Affirmations

These can help with anything from Little League to ballet class to memorizing lines for the school play.

- My arms and legs are under my control; my arms and legs are completely free.
- I am relaxed; I am focused. My attention doesn't waver.
- Breathing in, I'm relaxed; breathing out, I release all nervousness.
- This game (recital, play) is for my pleasure. My heart is filled with joy.

- My muscles are warm and relaxed; my muscles are firm and flexible.

Physical Meditation

In this kind of mindfulness, the objects of concentration are the limbs, extremities, and muscles of your own body. There are particular techniques designed to relieve stress and induce a meditative state, but any kind of physical activity will help.

The mind and body are not separate entities. Far from it. There's a close connection. Sports and exercises of various kinds can produce a meditative state of mind. This happens when endorphins are produced by the hypothalamus and other structures and then released into the bloodstream.

Endorphins are the body's natural opiates. They prevent pain impulses from reaching the brain and they induce that state of euphoria known famously as "runner's high." When produced during exercise, endorphins create a profound mental effect, leaving one bursting with self-confidence and self-esteem. Endorphins can help the mind develop a one-pointed focus much like mindfulness meditation.

Following are some of the techniques specifically designed to reduce stress, improve concentration, and even induce a state of bliss. One word of caution: Before doing any sport or physical activity, it's always wise to consult a physician or pediatrician. Make sure there's no reason to avoid physical activity before you begin.

Progressive Muscle Relaxation

With this technique, the goal is to tense and relax each muscle group in order from top to bottom or bottom to top. After being tensed, hard muscles will slacken, leaving you more relaxed and at peace. The repeated act of tensing and releasing muscles enables you to relax not only your body but your mind as well.

This process has a similar benefit to those described earlier in this chapter. Remember the monkey mind, the ceaseless chattering of our thoughts that are so ever-present as to be virtually unnoticeable? This can do great damage to our powers of concentration and our peace of mind.

Something similar happens in the body. In this high-speed, complicated world of ours, parents and children alike experience debilitating amounts of stress. One symptom is monkey mind; another symptom is physical tightness in many areas of the body. Tensing and releasing muscles allows you and your child to learn where you carry your tension. The more aware you become, the more you can relax your physical (and consequently your mental) tension throughout the day. Yes, children can learn this too. It will make a huge difference in the quality of their lives and the competence of their thought processes.

As always, begin by sitting comfortably. You can either have total silence or choose music that's appropriate to meditation. There's a lot of New Age music designed especially for relaxation and meditation. Smooth jazz and baroque classical are good choices. Stay away from music that's loud or drivingly rhythmical. This will interfere with the meditative mood.

This time, instead of focusing on your breath, you will focus on your right foot. Tense your foot. Feel the toes squeezing together. Now relax your right foot. Say to yourself, or even out loud, "My foot is relaxed. It's floating and sinking all at once. I can feel the muscles getting smoother and softer."

Move your attention to your calf. Do you feel any knots? Any soreness? Release the knots. Say to yourself, "My right calf is relaxed. It's floating and sinking all at once. I feel the muscles getting smoother and softer."

Hopefully you're feeling better already. Repeat this process with the rest of your body. Teach your child to do the same. After the calf, relax your right thigh, then your right hand, then your right arm. Do the same for your muscles on the left side.

As your muscles relax, your mind will relax with them. Now, focus on the tops of your shoulders. Say to yourself, "The tops of my shoulders are relaxed. They're floating and sinking at once. I feel the muscles getting smoother and softer." You may find yourself getting surprised. There are many places where we hold tension and don't even realize it.

Are you beginning to discover areas of your body that are tighter than you knew? Do you think it's any different for your child? It isn't. Don't be dismissive of your child's stress levels and the impact on his body and mind. Stress can be as debilitating in children as it is in adults.

Continue the relaxation process. Focus attention on your jaw. Say to yourself, "My jaw is relaxed. The muscles of my jaw are floating and sinking all at once. I feel the muscles getting smoother and softer." After this, tense and relax your eyelids.

After you've completed the progressive muscle relaxation you can repeat the process several times, or you can move into another form of meditation. Relaxing your muscles is a great way to start a longer session if this works for you and your child.

Yoga

Yoga has a very similar purpose as meditation. Today, we think of yoga as a form of physical exercise; but in its original form it was intended to train the mind as rigorously as it trains the body.

Yoga grew out of ancient Hindu practices. The word *yoga* means "to unite" or "to yoke." With what are we supposed to unite our minds? The ancient Hindus believed that by taking the body through a series of *asanas* (physical postures), we can release the everyday concerns of life and unite our minds with the divine. Some experts describe this as unifying the mind with God; others see it as an awakening to a universal consciousness.

Yoga and meditation have similar effects on the mind, whether or not we ascribe a mystical explanation to these practices. Many people undergo a change in consciousness that feels like the loss of one's everyday personality and a growing connection with something beyond our everyday lives.

You do not have to embrace the Hindu religion or a New Age belief system in order to have this experience. It's merely an effect of deep relaxation. If it happens to you or your child, just enjoy it. The only important thing to remember is that this is one way for you and your child to experience deep relaxation and total concentration. The benefits on mind-functioning can be outstanding.

Tai Chi

In twelfth-century China, so the legend says, Chan San-feng, a Shaolin monk, had a dream. He saw a crane fighting with a snake. The crane, like Chan himself, was a vigorous fighter, fierce, unyielding, and direct in his attack. With his beak the crane assaulted the snake, attempting to slay him. But the snake did not fight as the crane (Chan himself, perhaps?) expected. His attack was not direct. The snake slithered this way and that, escaping the crane's beak.

Instead of a direct attack, the snake, while evading the crane's deadly beak, struck the mighty bird with his tail. The crane had no chance to counter this indirect attack and he died instantly. The snake glided away, alive and victorious.

Chan San-feng arose from his dream with an insight. There was a new and better way to fight—one that eschewed direct attacks in favor of a more flexible, yielding approach. Warriors, Chan believed, would be more successful on the battlefield if they emulated the snake rather than the crane.

Thus, the art of tai chi was born. While it has its roots in the martial arts, tai chi today is used as a form of exercise. It's great for developing balance and, like yoga, can relax the mind and build up one's ability to concentrate.

Many (except for those with knee problems) find tai chi to be a less grueling form of body/mind training than yoga. *Tai* means "great" and *chi* can be translated as "system" or "ultimate reality"; the ancient Chinese, like the ancient Indians, sought a sense of connection with something beyond themselves. Again, whatever the explanation for this sense of altered reality, modern science is clear: Tai chi can offer many people improvements in physical and mental health.

Guided Imaging

Guided imaging or guided visualization is another technique that fosters a positive mind/body connection. This technique has helped athletes and actors, students and salesmen improve their performance. Educators and psychologists have used guided imaging to improve the academic performance of special education students and to treat children with emotional disturbances.

It is a powerful and often effective variation on meditation. Ancient Buddhist practitioners have developed complex and intricate imaging techniques on their path toward enlightenment. Even the present Dalai Lama uses guided imaging as part of his daily practice.

Contemporary individuals frequently use guided imaging, with great success, outside the world of Eastern religions. Here's a simple introduction to the technique:

Sit comfortably in a chair. Close your eyes (after you've read the next few paragraphs, of course). Imagine the chair is changing. It's no longer the club chair or kitchen chair you were using. Now you're sitting on a beach chair. Feel the flexible slats, the warm plastic. It's a hot day but there's no humidity. There's just the right amount of warmth to make you feel comfortable.

Your eyes are closed, but you can still see the scene in front of you. You are on a wide, white beach. The rolling waves beyond are the bluish-green of an unpolluted sea. You can hear the deep rush of the incoming waves. You hear them crash into the shore. You watch as the waves fade to a thin wash, darkening the line of sand right at the ocean's edge.

The sun is warm on your face. From time to time the warmth fades as a cool ocean breeze caresses your cheeks. Then the breeze dies down and the warmth returns. The sharp, salty smell of the sea fills your nostrils and mingles with the scent of coconut sunblock rising up from your skin.

Somewhere behind you a dog barks and children are laughing. In the distance, a radio is playing a baseball game. You hear the roar of a crowd over the radio, followed by the cheers of several men as they follow the game. A shadow blocks out the sun for a moment as a seagull, large and brilliantly white, passes overhead.

You're getting hotter and your mouth is drying out. You need a drink. Glancing down, you see a tall, amber glass of iced tea. You pick up the glass, feeling it's hard, cold surface. You take a sip and the sharp, sweet taste of the iced tea fills your mouth and then cools your throat. You take another sip, and another until your thirst is quenched. You sigh and a deep sense of contentment fills your body.

Do you realize what just happened to you? You've actually used every one of your physical senses during this exercise. Guided imaging is not just about pictures; it's about creating or re-creating an entire world with your mind and body. The poet Wordsworth once described poetry as being inspired by "emotion recollected in tranquility." This is very like the experience one has when doing guided imaging.

During a state of relaxation, one can create beautiful, peaceful images, involving any or all of the senses. This can reduce stress and deepen concentration in much the same way as other meditation techniques can. But guided imaging can do something else.

Coaches and CEOs know that guided imaging can be a path to peak performance. What you imagine can become a reality. This is good if your imagination runs to the positive. Unfortunately, many of us, adults and children alike, have negative images of the world and ourselves. This can carry us away from success toward disaster.

Depressed and anxious people are forever imagining a negative future, one where disasters happen and personal failures abound. Childhood is not always the stereotypical time of innocence and joy. Children often carry negative imagery around in their heads, and so do their parents.

A child who has experienced failure in school will approach learning with trepidation. She'll see herself failing future tests, embarrassing herself in front of her classmates, experiencing the disapproval and censure of her teacher and parents. Why study? Why try at all? Once such images fill her head, they become her living reality. To imagine oneself as a failure is to *be* a failure.

We can't just say "Try harder, dear." And heaven forbid we punish her. This will only add to the vicious cycle of incapacitating self-imaging. For many children and adults, the way out of this demoralizing maze is by practicing guided imaging. This alone will not make things better. Parents still need to focus on the learning strategies offered in this book, but guided imaging can help build a positive outlook that can potentially add to your child's success.

And your child doesn't have to be failing at school to benefit from guided imaging. People who are at the top of their game—sports figures, business leaders, and the like—use guided imaging to raise their already impressive skills to an even higher level. Guided imaging can serve as a competitive tool for the best and brightest.

There's one important idea to keep in mind. Teach your child to imagine that the scene is happening right here and now. We don't want to say "I wish this were true" or "Someday I will do the following." This carries the implication that we are not yet successful. Advocates of guided imaging insist that the best approach is to see ourselves living the success in the present.

Tailor the technique to your child's specific needs. Encourage her to visualize scenes in which she is succeeding at her academic goals. I've also suggested some visualizations below that your child might find helpful.

TEST-TAKING IMAGES

I'm sitting in class. Mrs. Crabbe, my teacher, has just put a test in front of me. I take a slow, deep breath and a warm, pleasant glow travels up from my toes. When the warmth reaches my face I begin to smile. I'm filled with confidence. I am sure I can remember everything.

I look at the first question. Suddenly, a door appears before my eyes. No one can see this door except me. Slowly, the door opens. I can hear it creak. Floating just inside is a piece of parchment paper. Words begin to form. Just like magic, the answer to the question appears.

Every time I look at a new question, the same thing happens. The door opens and the answer appears.

Mrs. Crabbe has given out the test. I can smell the paper and the ink. I read the first question. After I read it I hear a sound outside the window. A bird is singing. I look outside. The bird is shiny and golden. No one can see it or hear it except me. The bird's song turns into words. He is singing the answer to me! I look out the window and the bird winks at me. He's given me the answer and I know he's going to give me all the rest.

As your child sits and studies, ask her to imagine that her mind is a clay tablet. As she reviews a fact, a magic quill appears. It engraves that fact onto the tablet. She can feel the sharp cold point of the quill and the yielding softness of the clay tablet. She can also hear her own voice repeating the information as the quill is writing it down. As soon as the information is engraved on the tablet, your child can feel the clay hardening, fixing it permanently in her mind.

PERFORMANCE AND RECITATION IMAGES

Today, in Mrs. Crabbe's class, your child will be presenting an oral report. She stands in front of the class and looks at the back of the room. A cluster of soft, glowing lights appears as if from nowhere. The lights pulse and slowly take shape. There are people standing there, people with wings. A band of angels has arrived! Your child can feel a gentle breeze coming from their fluttering wings.

Mrs. Crabbe tells her to begin her report. The angels blow kisses. She can feel them touching her cheeks. As each kiss lands she can smell the scent of roses and feel peace spread from her face, down her spine, into her arms and down to her toes. Her whole body has turned into a vessel of peace.

She begins her report feeling calm and happy. Her voice comes out clear and confident.

Your child is in the class play (or the soccer game or the spelling bee or the marching band). She steps out in front of the audience. Their mouths aren't moving, yet she can hear inside their minds. Many of them are cheering silently. Others are saying things like "How talented she is!" or "What a winner!"

As soon as your child speaks or moves, she can feel a chill run up her spine. She is amazing! Somehow, she can feel everybody else's spine, too. They are all experiencing the same thrills and chills; everyone can feel your child's talent, including your child herself.

Today, Mrs. Crabbe is using flash cards to test everyone's knowledge of the multiplication tables. Every time your child sees one of the cards, she can see the back in her mind at the same time. She has a visual memory of all the answers. She can see the color and shape of the answers. She can see the position of each answer exactly as it's placed on the back of the card. When Mrs. Crabbe calls on her, the answer appears immediately, and in a calm, clear voice she calls out the answer.

These are just a few examples of guided imaging. The goal of these is to reduce stress and to activate the memory. This is a skill like any other, and the more your child practices the better she'll become. Make sure the images you use inspire her. Try as many of these as you can think of until you find one or two that work best for your child.

CHAPTER 5

Building Background Knowledge with
Idiomatic Expressions

Many English language learners find our language difficult because of its vast sea of idiomatic expressions. An idiom is a phrase that conveys a meaning beyond what the literal words say. In fact, if one doesn't grasp the import of the idiom, the words themselves can seem no more than so much mumbo-jumbo.

When children aren't exposed to idiomatic expressions, or when adults don't use and explain them, this can become a barrier to reading comprehension. Authors don't sit around worrying about whether your child knows many of the common idioms of our language. They assume (mostly unconsciously) that readers will understand these phrases, as they are part of our common linguistic culture.

One way to enrich your child's background knowledge is to expose him to as many idiomatic expressions as possible. Following are some of the most common. The list is not exhaustive. But this selection will certainly enrich your child's knowledge and appreciation of the quirky treasures to be found in the English language.

One thing: *Please* don't force your child to sit around memorizing this list. He'll never retain most of it that way. Instead, pick the ones you like and simply find opportunities to use them when talking with your child. He will then pick up on the ones he likes best and in time might start using these expressions in his own dialogue. At the very least, he will recognize the phrases and their meanings when they appear in books and conversations.

Encourage your child to delight in language. Don't test him on these idiomatic expressions. If you do, the pleasure of using language well could feel more like a burden. Idioms should be vital and enjoyable jewels of expression.

Following are some of the most common idiomatic expressions in English:

Absent-minded:
A person is said to be absent-minded when he's forgetful.

Ace up one's sleeve:
A person is said to have an ace up her sleeve when she has unexpected information or an unexpected skill that will give her the upper hand in a situation.

A hop, skip, and a jump:
When you're traveling to a place, if it's only a hop, skip, and a jump from your present location, then it's very close.

Airing one's dirty laundry:
When people discuss their personal, private, and most unsavory problems publicly, they are said to be airing their dirty laundry.

All ears:
When you are paying close attention or listening carefully to someone else, you are all ears.

As the crow flies:
The straightest distance and shortest traveling time from one location to the next is the time it takes to get to your destination "as the crow flies."

At each other's throats:
When two people are angry and constantly arguing, they are at each other's throats.

At the drop of a hat:
If somebody decides to do something at the drop of a hat, it means she'll do it impulsively and immediately.

Ax to grind:
If someone has an ax to grind, that means his actions have a hidden negative motive, such as resentment or revenge.

Backhanded compliment:
When someone, on the surface, appears to be giving a compliment but an insult is implied, that's a backhanded compliment: "You look lovely today, dear. I hardly recognized you."

Beat around the bush:
In a conversation, if someone is uncomfortable about coming right out with a piece of information or about bringing up a difficult topic, and instead talks about all sorts of related things first, then he's said to be beating around the bush.

Bend over backward:
If someone will make every effort to help another person, no matter how difficult helping her might be, then he's bending over backward to help her.

Black market:
When someone purchases something illegally (and for less than the going rate) she is said to have bought it on the black market. (Your child should be told that this is an idea, not a real place.)

Black sheep of the family:
The black sheep of a family is the person who is different from the rest of the family and/or rejected by them. A black sheep can be one who often gets into trouble, or it can be a person who has different social or political views from the rest of the family.

Blow one's own horn:
When a person boasts about himself, he is said to be blowing (or tooting) his own horn.

Bolt from the blue:
When something happens or some information arrives that is completely unexpected, like lightning on a clear afternoon, it's called a bolt from the blue.

Bootleg:
A product (such as a movie or a Gucci bag) that has been copied and sold illegally is a bootleg.

Bottom line:
In business and in human transactions generally, when one is concerned primarily with the profits that an activity will yield, one is concerned with the bottom line.

Break the ice:
When people in a social situation are uncomfortable, and someone says or does something that makes everyone relax and gets them talking, that person has broken the ice.

Breathe down someone's neck:
If somebody is constantly watching and judging an activity you are doing, or if she is constantly in your business, she is breathing down your neck.

Breath of fresh air:
If somebody brings a new perspective to a situation or if she livens things up, she is said to be a breath of fresh air.

Bricks-and-mortar store:
When you go to an actual, physical location to make a purchase, as opposed to buying the item online, you are shopping at a bricks-and-mortar store.

Bring the house down:
When you perform successfully and people are cheering wildly, you have brought the house down.

Bury one's head in the sand:
When a person tries to ignore a situation because it makes him uncomfortable, then like an ostrich he is burying his head in the sand in the hope that what he can't see, can't see him.

Bury the hatchet:
When two people who don't get along agree to treat each other better and stop arguing, they have buried the hatchet.

Catch someone's drift:
Once somebody begins to understand and like your point of view or your unique way of doing things, he has caught your drift.

Caught red-handed:
Caught in the act: If someone is stealing and you actually see her doing it, she's been caught red-handed.

Chasing rainbows:
If you are trying to make an impossible dream come true, you are chasing rainbows.

Chip off the old block:
If your personality or behavior is just like that of your mother or father, then you're a chip off the old block.

Chip on one's shoulder:
A person with a combative or arrogant attitude is said to have a chip on her shoulder.

Clear the air:
When people have a discussion to resolve their disagreements and misunderstandings with each other in order to get along better in the future, they've cleared the air.

Close shave:

If you nearly got in trouble but escaped unharmed, that was a close shave.

Cold shoulder:

When you avoid someone and refuse to talk to him, you're giving him the cold shoulder.

Cook one's goose:

When something happens that gets you into serious trouble, your goose is cooked.

Costs a pretty penny:

If something is expensive, it costs a pretty penny.

Couch potato:

Somebody who sits around watching TV and never gets any exercise is a couch potato.

Crying over spilled milk:

If you're constantly worrying about a past situation instead of getting on with your life, you're crying over spilled milk.

Cutting corners:

Doing something quickly and cheaply (and possibly creating an unsafe situation) means that you are cutting corners.

Dark horse:

When a person who is unlikely to succeed comes out on top, she is the dark horse.

Dead wood:

When a person holds others back from succeeding because he isn't doing his part, he is dead wood.

Dolled up:

A woman who is elaborately dressed to impress is all dolled up.

Drag one's feet:

If you are obligated to do something but you don't want to do it, you may get to it as slowly as possible. You are therefore dragging your feet.

Dressed to the nines:

When you're dressed up fancy, you're dressed to the nines.

Drop-dead gorgeous:

When someone is so good looking that he makes you feel like your heart has skipped a beat, that person is drop-dead gorgeous.

Drop off:

Dropping off means falling asleep, in or out of bed.

Drop off the face of the earth:

When someone hasn't been seen, or has removed himself from his social circle, for a long time, he's said to have dropped off the face of the earth.

Eat one's words:

If you have to apologize for something you've said, or take back an opinion that turned out to be wrong, you will be eating your words.

Eighty-six it:

If you put an end to a plan, or kill it, you've eighty-sixed it.

Elbow room:

If you have enough room to move physically, or if you've been given the leeway to move ahead with a plan of yours, you've been given elbow room.

Fair-weather friend:

Somebody who is your friend in good times, but deserts you during bad times, is a fair-weather friend.

Feather in one's cap:
An accomplishment for which you can take credit is a feather in your cap.

Fell off the back of a truck:
When used to describe where clothing or other goods came from, this means they were stolen. (Your child should know that this doesn't refer to a real truck.)

Fifth wheel:
Somebody who is extra or unnecessary in a job or social setting is the fifth wheel.

Find one's sea legs:
When you begin to feel competent in a social or business setting, you've found your sea legs.

Flying by the seat of one's pants:
When you do things spontaneously without having a well-thought-out plan, you're flying by the seat of your pants.

Fly in the ointment:
The fly in the ointment is the person or circumstance that prevents an endeavor from working out satisfactorily.

Fly off the handle:
When you get angry quickly and easily, often for little or no reason, you are flying off the handle.

Foam at the mouth:
A person who is so angry that she seems to be out of control or even crazy is said to be, like a rabid dog, foaming at the mouth.

Food for thought:
When something is very interesting and worth mulling over, it becomes food for thought.

Fork in the road:

When a road splits in two directions, you've come to a fork in the road. This is my personal favorite because I remember traveling into the country with my parents when I was very small and looking for a piece of cutlery embedded in the ground. My mother was reading directions and told my father to look for a fork in the road and go right.

From hand to mouth:

When you can never save money, when you earn barely enough to survive from day to day, you're living from hand to mouth.

Front-runner:

The person who is most likely to win in an election is called the front-runner.

Gathering dust:

When something has been ignored and unused for a long time, it is said to be gathering dust.

Get away with murder:

When someone does something wrong and profits from it, he has gotten away with murder. (Your child should know that this is not a literal reference to murder.)

Get down to brass tacks:

When you're talking about the basic facts or essentials of a matter, you've gotten down to brass tacks.

Get our wires crossed:

There has been a miscommunication. You and someone else have misunderstood which of you will be responsible for a particular activity; or you think you've been talking about the same thing when you each have a different meaning in your head. You have gotten your wires crossed.

Get reamed out:
When you have been severely reprimanded, you've been reamed out.

Get something off the ground:
When you get a project started, you've gotten it off the ground.

Get the hang of something:
Learning how to do something—beginning to develop a skill—means getting the hang of it.

Get wind of something:
When you find out about something (usually something secret) through indirect sources, you've gotten wind of it.

Given the green light:
When you get permission to begin a project, you've been given the green light to go. Children should understand that this is related to the green light signal that means "Go" for automotive traffic.

Going overboard:
When someone is too enthusiastic about or obsessed with an endeavor, she's gone overboard.

Good head on one's shoulders:
If you have common sense, you've got a good head on your shoulders.

Gray area:
When something is not clearly good or bad, or right or wrong, this in-between area is called a gray area.

Green thumb:
If you're good at growing plants, you've got a green thumb.

Handling something with kid gloves:
When a situation requires all your diplomacy, you must handle it with (protective) kid gloves.

Having a full plate:
When you are so busy you cannot take on another task, your plate is full.

Having one's hands full:
Having many obligations or demands that you must deal with at the same time means that you have your hands full.

Having one's hands tied:
When circumstances prevent you from changing a situation, your hands are tied.

Heard it through the grapevine:
If people in your social circle are gossiping about something—especially if it's something that you weren't meant to know about—and they share the information with you, you heard it through the grapevine.

Hot potato:
When a situation is so sensitive that nobody wants to deal with it for fear of painful consequences, it's a hot potato.

Hot under the collar:
Somebody who is really angry, so much so that he's getting red in the face, is hot under the collar.

In a nutshell:
If you've gotten (or given) a clear, concise summary of a situation or story, you've gotten it (or given it) in a nutshell.

In the nick of time:
If a task has been completed shortly before failure or even disaster might have occurred, you've completed the task in the nick of time.

In the pipeline:
A project that is in progress and working its way through the various stages to completion is in the pipeline.

Jack-of-all-trades:
Also: jack of all trades, master of none. If you have a little bit of skill in a lot of areas but you've never become an expert in any one of those areas, you're a jack-of-all-trades.

Jerk me around:
If you're telling me lies and leading me on, then you're jerking me around.

Jump on the bandwagon:
When you join a popular cause or trend, you have jumped on the bandwagon.

Just what the doctor ordered:
Getting exactly what you need to feel good or to improve an undesirable situation is getting just what the doctor ordered.

Keep a low profile:
When you don't offer your opinions or call attention to yourself because you think it might bring trouble, then you're keeping a low profile.

Keep it under your hat:
You're keeping something under your hat if you're keeping it secret.

Keep one's ear to the ground:
When you're keeping your ear to the ground, you are keeping alert for any rumors or information that affect your situation.

Keep one's eyes peeled:
See *keep one's ear to the ground,* above, but for visual warning signs. You can use either sense to achieve the same goal.

Keep one's nose clean:
If you're avoiding trouble, you're keeping your nose clean.

Keep one's nose to the grindstone:
Working hard or studying hard and not allowing yourself to be distracted—that's keeping your nose to the grindstone.

Kill two birds with one stone:
If you have found a way to accomplish two tasks or solve two problems at the same time, you've killed two birds with one stone.

Knock me down with a feather:
When you're totally shocked and surprised, you could be knocked down with a feather.

Know on which side your bread is buttered:
If you're sharp and you know which people can help you succeed or prosper, you know where your bread is buttered.

Land on your feet:
When you survive a difficult situation, you have landed on your feet.

Lay down the law:
When you've told someone the rules in very strong terms, you've laid down the law.

Lead down (or up) the garden path:
Someone who has deceived you has led you down (or up) a garden path.

Learning the ropes:
In any new job, you need to learn the basic competencies needed for success. As you are gaining these competencies, you are learning the ropes.

Left wing:
If you have very liberal or modern views, you have a left-wing outlook.

Lend an ear:
You lend an ear to someone when you listen sympathetically to her talking about her troubles.

Like a duck to water:
If you discover that you really love a new activity and you're naturally very good at it, you've taken to it like a duck to water.

Like a fish out of water:
When you're in an uncomfortable, unfamiliar situation, you may feel like a fish out of water.

Like a moth to a flame:
If you are attracted to a risky situation or to a person who can only bring trouble, you are attracted like a moth to a flame.

Like finding a needle in a haystack:
Looking for someone or something that is hard to locate is like trying to find a needle in a haystack.

Lip service:
When somebody pretends to agree with an idea or position but doesn't really mean what they're saying, that person is giving lip service to the idea.

Living the life of Riley:
When you have a comfortable life with a lot of money and material possessions, you're living the life of Riley.

Look daggers at someone:
Somebody who looks at you with great anger and malevolence—so fiercely that it seems he could kill you with just one glance—is looking daggers at you.

Look down your nose at somebody:
If you act superior to another person, you're looking down your nose at her.

Lose one's marbles:
If someone is very confused or perhaps even suffering from mental illness, then it can be said that they've lost their marbles.

Mad about somebody:
Also: crazy for somebody. This expression means that you like this person a lot.

Make ends meet:
When the money you've earned is sufficient to pay your bills, but no more, you've made ends meet.

Make mincemeat out of someone:
If you've chastised and humiliated someone, you've made mincemeat out of them.

Make one's flesh crawl:
When something scares you and gives you goosebumps, it makes your flesh crawl.

Make tracks:
You're making a quick exit—making tracks out of there.

Mind like a sieve:
A person with a poor memory or one who is absent-minded has a mind like a sieve.

Muddy the waters:
When somebody makes a situation more confusing, they've muddied the waters.

Mum's the word:
When you agree to keep a secret, mum's the word.

Music to one's ears:

When you've gotten an agreement or when you've been told exactly what you want to hear; it's music to your ears.

Never darken my door:

If you never want to see or hear from someone again, tell them to never darken your door again.

No love lost:

When two people dislike each other, there's no love lost between them.

Off the hook:

This is one of my pet peeves. So many teachers I know use this phrase when their classes have been out of control. "Off the hook" does not mean "out of control." If you're off the hook it means you were previously in trouble but you got out of it.

Off the record:

When you provide someone with confidential information, but you're unwilling to admit it publicly, you've provided the information off the record.

Off the top of one's head:

Saying something without planning or mulling it over in advance is speaking off the top of your head.

Off the wall:

Someone who is out of control and acting a bit crazy is off the wall. People often misuse the term "off the hook" when they mean to say "off the wall."

Once in a blue moon:

When something happens only on very rare occasions, it happens once in a blue moon.

On nodding terms:

When you know someone by sight but you've never spoken to her or gotten to know her well, you're on nodding terms.

On one's high horse:

Someone who is very conceited and acting superior to others is on his high horse.

On pins and needles:

If you're in a state of suspense, you're on pins and needles.

On the back burner:

If you decide to put off a project for a while, you're putting it on the back burner.

On the ball:

When somebody is knowledgeable and prepared and knows how to handle himself in a challenging situation, he is on the ball.

On the house:

If a restaurant or store gives you something for free, it's on the house.

On the level:

Someone who is honest with you is being on the level.

On the same wavelength:

If you and somebody else think the same way or hold the same beliefs, then you're on the same wavelength.

Open a can of worms:

When you broach a difficult subject or involve yourself in a complicated situation, you've opened a can of worms.

Out of this world:

Something that is really wonderful is out of this world.

Out on a limb:
When you take a risk, you go out on a limb.

Out to lunch:
When someone is eccentric or downright crazy—or just spaced out in a world of her own—you might consider her out to lunch.

Over the hill:
Someone who is getting on in years and not as sharp as he used to be is sometimes said to be over the hill. It's not the most respectful of phrases; so warn your children that you'll feel insulted if they refer to you as over the hill.

Pass the buck:
When you refuse to accept responsibility, you have passed the buck.

Picking up the pieces:
When your life has come through a crisis and you take steps to make it better, you're picking up the pieces.

Piece of cake:
If something is really easy for you to do, it's a piece of cake.

Poker face:
If you're in a challenging situation and you don't show your emotions, you've got a poker face.

Pull someone's leg:
Someone who is telling an untruth as a joke or a playful trick is pulling your leg.

Pull strings:
Someone who uses her influence to help you gain an advantage is pulling strings.

Pull your punches:

When someone gives you a scolding or a reprimand but goes easy on you, he's pulling his punches.

Put in your two cents:

When you give your opinion, you're putting in your two cents.

Put one's foot in one's mouth:

If you say something or voice an opinion that causes embarrassment for yourself, you've put your foot in your mouth.

Put someone on the spot:

When you embarrass another person by forcing her to discuss or confess something she doesn't want to discuss, or when you make a request of someone that she wishes she could refuse, you've put her on the spot.

Put your best foot forward:

When you publicly demonstrate your talents or when you've dressed up to look your best, you've put your best foot forward.

Race against time:

If you have little time to complete a task, you're in a race against time.

Railroad:

When you force someone into a situation or create a situation where an innocent person gets into trouble, you've railroaded her.

Raining cats and dogs:

If it's raining heavily, it's raining cats and dogs.

Red tape:

When you're dealing with a lot of complicated rules and regulations and forms, you have to "cut through the red tape" to get anything done.

Ride someone's coattails:

If you ally yourself with a successful person in order to gain your own success, you're riding the other person's coattails.

Right wing:

If you have very conservative or old-fashioned views, you have a right-wing outlook.

Rings a bell:

When a face or a name is familiar but you can't quite remember the person, then his face or name has rung a bell.

Rude awakening:

When someone has discovered in the harshest possible way that her behavior has brought her trouble, she's had a rude awakening.

See eye to eye:

Two people who agree or have the same point of view are seeing eye to eye.

Sell like hotcakes:

A product that sells quickly and in great quantities is said to be selling like hotcakes.

Send someone packing:

When you fire an employee or demand that someone get out of your life, you've sent him packing.

Shout-out:

Publicly thanking someone is giving her a shout-out.

Smooth someone's ruffled feathers:

When someone is angry and you're trying to calm him down, you're smoothing his feathers.

Sour grapes:
Someone who envies your good fortune but belittles it because she didn't have your luck is suffering from sour grapes.

Spill the beans:
When you give away a secret, you've spilled the beans.

Splitting hairs:
In an argument or discussion, if you make a big deal out of small, unimportant details, you're splitting hairs.

Spread like wildfire:
If news or gossip reaches many people in a short amount of time, it's spreading like wildfire.

Square peg in a round hole:
If someone doesn't fit into a social situation because he's very different in outlook or behavior from the rest, that person is like a square peg in a round hole. In other words, he doesn't fit.

Sticky fingers:
A person with sticky fingers can't keep her hands off other people's property—she's a thief.

Stone's throw:
A location that is nearby is only a stone's throw away.

Straight from the horse's mouth:
This is the opposite of gossip, which you hear indirectly through others. If you've heard something from the horse's mouth, the person who is directly involved in a situation has given you the facts.

Take a load off:
When you ask a visitor to sit down and relax, you've asked him to take a load off (his feet, that is).

Take something in one's stride:
If you deal with a difficult situation competently and without getting upset, you've taken it in your stride.

Take something with a grain of salt:
If you don't completely trust the accuracy of someone's information and so don't take it too seriously, then you've taken it with a grain of salt.

Take the bull by the horns:
By taking charge of a tough situation, you've taken the bull by the horns.

Take the wind out of someone's sails:
When you say something that obliterates a person's enthusiasm, you've knocked the wind out of his sails.

Take your hat off to someone:
When you congratulate someone, you take your hat off to her. (Tipping one's hat used to be a sign of respect.)

Thick as thieves:
Two people who are extremely close can be called thick as thieves.

Think on one's feet:
If you can respond quickly in a difficult situation, without having to sit down and puzzle out a solution, you can think on your feet.

Thorn in one's side:
A person who is constantly irritating is a thorn in your side.

Tickled pink:
When you're really delighted by something, you're tickled pink.

Top dog:
The leader or the person in charge is the top dog.

Turn a blind eye:

If you ignore another person's wrongdoing, you are turning a blind eye to it.

Turn the tables:

If a situation with another person is not going your way and you change it to your advantage, you have turned the tables.

Two-faced:

Someone who acts like your friend but works against your interests when your back is turned is two-faced.

Underdog:

In a competition, the person who appears least likely to come out on top is the underdog.

Vote with one's feet:

When you show your disapproval by refusing to participate in an objectionable situation, or when you no longer give someone your business because they've offended you, then you are voting with your feet.

Watch somebody like a hawk:

When you're paying close attention to someone's activities because you don't trust her, you're watching her like a hawk.

Went through the roof:

This can have two different meanings, one negative and one positive. If somebody gets really angry, he's gone through the roof. Alternately, if something sells very well and earns a lot of profits, that item has gone through the roof.

Without batting an eyelash:

If you do or say something difficult without showing that you're stressed out, you're doing it without batting an eyelash.

CHAPTER 6

Building Background Knowledge with
Popular Proverbs and **Sayings**

Here's your chance: a way to enrich your child's language skills and to teach her moral values at the same time. Proverbs and sayings have long been used as instructional devices. Like the mnemonic devices you will learn about in the next two chapters, proverbs are used to remember complex ideas quickly and easily.

In this case, the complex ideas involve hoped-for behavioral norms. Just like idiomatic expressions, proverbs and wise sayings shouldn't be memorized. They are rich linguistic treasures but they have no value if they are detached from life through meaningless memorization or recitation.

Consult the list often, and use some of the sayings when the opportunity arises. Encourage others in your family to use them, too. It's less important to use every saying on the list than it is to use the ones that you find meaningful and applicable to actual events in your family.

Following are some of the most popular proverbs and sayings. I'm sure you know others. Expose your child to those, too.

A chain is only as strong as its weakest link.
If a team, or group with a common goal, is working together, everyone must do their best in order to achieve at the highest level.

A picture is worth a thousand words.
Long explanations aren't always useful. Seeing something for your-self will teach you more than an explanation will.

Actions speak louder than words.
People often claim that they are going to do something good. The real proof of your goodness, however, is not the claims you make but the acts you perform.

All things grow with time, except for grief.
When we are grieving, it's hard to believe that our suffering will ever end. If we are patient, however, we can take comfort in know-ing that our grief will fade. Grief, unlike positive things, such as love and friendship, grows weaker with every passing day.

An empty purse frightens away friends.
Many people act like friends until we have financial troubles in our lives. Then those friends stop seeing us.

An ounce of prevention is worth a pound of cure.
If you do small things to prevent problems, you won't have to do big things when the problems arise. For example, following a good diet prevents a lot of diseases. It is better, then, to follow the diet now than to deal with a life-threatening disease in the future.

A fool and his money are soon parted.
People who are careless can be tricked into giving away their money.

A friend in need is a friend indeed.
Friends who have fallen on hard times may use their friendship to get help from you—maybe even monetary help.

A good beginning makes a good end.
If you make a serious effort to succeed, and don't put it off until later, you are likely to achieve your goal.

A person is known by the company he keeps.

Our reputation (good or bad) is based not only on our actions but on our associations. If we associate with negative people, others will view us in a negative light. If we associate with respectable people, others will respect us.

A smooth sea never made a skilled sailor.

Unless we are brave enough to face and deal with difficulties, we will never become good at solving life's problems.

A stitch in time saves nine.

A small tear in a piece of cloth will become a big rip if you don't sew it right away; and a small problem will become a big problem if you don't deal with it as soon as it arises.

As you sow, so shall you reap.

If you do good things, you will gather rewards. If you do bad things, you will bring trouble into your world.

It's better to be alone than in bad company.

If you associate with bad people, your life will be filled with trouble. If you do the right thing, even if no one joins you, you will earn self-respect.

Better late than never.

If you haven't made an effort to achieve your goals, you can still experience success if you start right now.

Birds of a feather flock together.

People from the same background or with the same point of view tend to associate with each other rather than with those who are different.

Don't count your chickens before they hatch.

If you have set goals and you haven't yet achieved them, don't count on them. For example, if you've made an investment but you haven't made money on it yet, don't go shopping based on the expectation that you will be able to pay later. You may wind up in debt.

Don't judge a book by its cover.

Unless you really know someone, don't judge them by their appearance. They may be very different from the prejudices you've formed in your mind.

Don't put off till tomorrow what you can do today.

If you have an obligation, take care of it as soon as possible because you don't know what other obligations might arise. If you wait, you might not have time to complete the task later on.

Experience is the father of wisdom.

The more people you meet and the more situations you deal with, the wiser you'll be at meeting life's challenges.

Faint heart never won fair lady.

If you're shy, you won't gain the affection of the person you like. Speak up for yourself and show your feelings.

Give him an inch and he'll take a mile.

If you let someone take advantage of you, he will continue to do it and take greater and greater liberties.

Half a loaf is better than none.

People make themselves miserable by whining over the things they don't have. You'll get greater pleasure out of life if you appreciate the things you already have.

Haste makes waste.
If you rush into a task and do it carelessly, you may mess it up. Then you'll lose time and profits because you'll have to do it all over again.

He who laughs last laughs best.
Somebody may gloat because they've beaten you; but if you turn the tables and succeed after all, you get to enjoy your victory even more than the other guy enjoyed his.

He who plays with fire gets burned.
If you become involved in dangerous situations or associate with bad people, you will wind up getting hurt.

Home is where the heart is.
Sometimes our biological families are not the people we love best. Other people might be kinder and more supportive. These are the people we love, and wherever they can be found, that's our true home. Also, if there's an activity we love, wherever we can participate in that activity is the home of our heart.

It takes two to tango.
If someone attempts to argue with you and you walk away, then the argument is over. You both have to participate to keep the argument going.

Look before you leap.
Don't take careless risks. Consider the consequences before you say or do something you might regret.

Loose lips sink ships.
Gossip is not a harmless sport. It can cause a lot of trouble and unhappiness to others. Gossip can prevent people from reaching a collective goal if it causes them to argue.

Many hands make light work.
Many tasks are easier to accomplish through teamwork.

Necessity is the mother of invention.
People can get very creative when they have a problem they must solve.

No news is good news.
If we're worried that we might hear some bad news but we haven't heard anything yet, then there's room for hope.

Nothing ventured, nothing gained.
If we don't take reasonable risks in life, we'll reap no rewards.

Once bitten, twice shy.
If you've had a bad experience, you'll do anything to avoid a similar experience.

One man's meat is another man's poison.
We might find an experience pleasant or useful, while someone else might find it disagreeable. We shouldn't assume that others will feel the same way about things as we do.

People who live in glass houses shouldn't throw stones.
Think twice before you criticize other people. Your attack might call attention to similar faults of your own and open you up to the criticism of others.

Practice makes perfect.
In order to become good at a skill, we must keep practicing.

Practice what you preach.
Some people are very good at telling others how to behave without behaving that way themselves. An honorable person will follow his own rules of behavior.

The apple doesn't fall far from the tree.
People behave much the same way that their parents behave.

Too many cooks spoil the broth.
If too many people try to be in charge, there will be so much conflict and confusion that success will be difficult to achieve.

Variety is the spice of life.
Life is more interesting and exciting when you associate with people who have different ideas and backgrounds.

When the cat's away the mice will play.
If your teacher or your mother is not around, you're likely to do things you normally wouldn't be permitted to do. Without a supervisor, people can become lazy or troublemakers.

When in Rome, do as the Romans do.
If you're in a new environment, learn the customs and try to fit in. You might offend people if you fail to learn their social rules.

You can catch more flies with honey than with vinegar.
Constantly criticizing people will not lead to success. Try complimenting them instead. You might get more cooperation.

Where there's a will there's a way.
No matter what the obstacle, if you're determined to overcome it, you'll find a way to do it.

CHAPTER 7

Memory Games

Some people have prodigious memories. Most of us do not. Others have great memories for some things but not for others. I, for example, can quote Shakespeare and Chaucer from memory and can recite famous lines from hundreds of movies, books, and songs. But heaven help you if you rely on me to remember driving directions from one location to the next.

You wouldn't expect a piano student to play a sonata without learning keyboarding techniques. You wouldn't let a child compete at softball without teaching her how to pitch, catch, and use a bat. The same goes for memory. We shouldn't expect children to retain information without teaching them how to remember.

In Chapter 1, you read how children retain information while reading. In this chapter, you will learn a variety of techniques that will help your child (and you) recall information with greater efficiency. They work by helping your child:

- Classify ideas in groups
- Make connections between various bits of information
- Activate the five senses
- Use creativity to deepen understanding of a topic

Matching "War"

Remember the popular card game War? You can create your own variation for any topic your child needs to study. I'll give two examples, one for science and one for grammar. Suppose your child needs to learn the difference between creatures that are mammals and those that are not. Mammals, you'll remember, are warm-blooded and feed milk to their young.

Download pictures of various creatures or cut them out of magazines. You can even go to the zoo or your local pet store to take photographs. Then make a trip to your local office supply store for washable glue sticks and card stock. With your child, glue the pictures to the card stock and write the name of the animal on the back. In parentheses, ask her to write "mammal" or "not mammal" with a brief explanation of why the creature in question is or isn't a mammal. For example:

- **Whale:** "Mammal" (Warm-blooded, the female feeds milk to her young.)
- **Trout:** "Not a mammal" (Cold-blooded, the female does not produce milk.)
- **Kangaroo:** "Mammal" (Warm-blooded, the female feeds milk to her young.)
- **Human being:** "Mammal" (Warm-blooded, the female feeds milk to her young.)
- **Salamander:** "Not a mammal" (Cold-blooded, the female does not produce milk.)
- **Cat:** "Mammal" (Warm-blooded, the female feeds milk to her young.)

Produce at least thirty of these cards, more if you're going to play with large groups. Toss a pair of dice to see who goes first. The highest number begins. Then go clockwise as each player gets a turn.

Shuffle the deck and give each player five cards. Then turn up a card from the deck and put it in the center of the table. If player 1 is holding a mammal card in his hand, and the card turned up is a mammal, he can match it with his mammal card, pick both up, and put them aside.

If the card isn't a mammal card (is a snake, for instance) and player 1 has only mammal cards then player 1 one can do nothing. Each player has a turn until someone can take the snake. If no one can pick it up in the first round, turn up a new card from the deck and repeat until somebody can go.

The aim is to get rid of all your cards. The first player to do so wins. While playing War, each person has to make a connection between those creatures that are mammals and those that are not. A pattern is formed in the player's mind, and this pattern activates memory. You can include additional categories, such as reptiles and amphibians, for older children. The game can get more and more advanced as your children do.

This game can be played with a whole variety of subjects—grammar, for example. Instead of living creatures, the cards could include words such as the following:

- Cat
- Car
- Green
- Beautiful
- Threw
- Graceful
- Secretly
- Disdainfully
- Dances

Have you caught on? The players would have to group their cards according to which are nouns, verbs, adjectives, and adverbs. The game of War can go on and on, teaching your child the connections between all sorts of facts and ideas. Be creative and include your child in the constructing of the cards. Instead of the dreaded "drill and kill," your child can experience memorization as a game.

Writing an Informational Book

This is a great way to learn through classification. It also links reading and writing, which aids memory. With your child, look at age-appropriate magazines and informational books, even textbooks. Together, examine how books are broken into chapters and how articles are broken into sections with tiles.

Fold paper into a booklet. Create a title page with appropriate cover art (drawn or cut and pasted). Make sure the name of the author—your child—is on the cover, too.

Then the two of you can discuss how to break the topic into chapters. If, for example, your child is writing about *biomes* (various living environments), he might create chapters on:

- Deserts
- Grasslands
- Tropical rain forests
- Tundra
- Deciduous forests
- Coniferous forests

Each chapter will have subsections (with subheadings and appropriate illustrations and captions) on plant life, animal life, the climate, etc. As your child writes what he knows about each, he will see the connections and differences among them. And if his teacher is open to it, this might make a great extra-credit assignment!

Fact Narratives

A narrative, or story, tells events in chronological order. In a fact narrative, your child will invent a tale in which important facts are encountered along the way. Suppose, in social studies, Mr. Bovine is teaching world religions. Your child might have to memorize the names of world religions and say whether or not they are monotheistic, polytheistic, or neither. Create a silly story like the following:

Last weekend was smoking! My uncle, Angus Dei, took me shopping in that new retail store in the mall, Gods R Us. Who do you think we ran into? It was Homer, the famous poet. He was carrying a whole bunch of boxes with one arm. He nearly dropped them several times because his Seeing Eye dog kept tugging at the leash. Every time the dog tugged, Homer and his boxes would wobble.

"Homer, what are you doing here?" I asked. "And what's in the boxes?"

"Well," said Homer, "I'm performing at a middle school next week and I had to buy models of all the ancient Greek gods and goddesses to show examples from my polytheistic religion. The

Zeus model is really cool. Look, he has changeable thunderbolts in different glow-in-the-dark colors."

No sooner did we say goodbye to Homer than we ran into our neighbor Sr. Jesus deJesus. He was carrying a large crate with a big "M" pasted to the side. Inside were a lot of small boxes. Each of these also had an "M" on its side.

"This is my Christianity box," Sr. deJesus said. "It's one big box because Christianity believes in one God."

"That means it's monotheistic," I said.

"Right," said Sr. deJesus.

"But what are those smaller boxes?" I asked.

"Well," said my neighbor, "there are different forms of Christianity inside the one big box. See that one? It's Roman Catholicism. And that one is the Baptist box. The Lutheran box is right next to it."

"And what are all those small boxes that look like ring boxes?"

"There are many independent Pentecostal churches," Sr. deJesus said. "Those are just some of them."

We bid him goodbye and turned into another aisle. There were two men in orange robes.

"Hey," said Uncle Angus, "I know those guys. They're Buddhist monks from different schools."

"The one on the left is lazy," I said. "He's letting the other one carry all the boxes while he carries none."

"Each one is carrying his own gods," Uncle Angus said. "The one on the left sees Buddhism as a philosophy and not a religion, so he doesn't embrace any gods. The fellow on the right, however, is carrying a whole bunch of traditional deities."

"So it's just like Christianity," I said. "There are many belief systems within the one big system."

"Yes," said Uncle Angus, "religion is a melting pot, just like our nation."

If you and your child were to tell this story over and over, just for the fun of it, come test time she would remember most, if not all, of the information on world religions. Verbal-linguistic children will love this technique. You can add in sound effects and visual descriptions if this helps make the activity more fun.

Timelines

These are most commonly found in social studies lessons to illustrate important events, such as the major battles of World War II, but timelines can be used in a variety of ways. Timelines can be used to:

- Memorize math and science formulas
- Memorize and explain scientific procedures
- Review major plot points in a book

Timelines can help children (and adults) organize and absorb information. When your child is learning a math or science formula, ask her to place each step on a sentence strip. (You can get them at office supply stores and teacher stores.) Tape the timeline to a wall. Whenever she tries a specific problem, ask her to consult the timeline as she completes the formula.

After she's done this several times, ask her to close her eyes and try to see the timeline without looking at it. With repeated practice, many children can begin to visualize such timelines in their heads. Then, on a test it will be easier to remember important formulas.

In some states, standardized tests now require students to explain their mathematical or scientific reasoning in words. Even if your child gets the answer right, she will lose points if she cannot explain her thinking.

Timelines can help. Ask your child to place some of her math problems or steps of a science experiment on a timeline. Causes of historical incidents can be timelined, too. Ask her to turn each point on the line into a sentence. When she's finished, she will likely have a clear explanation of her work.

Okay, okay, I can hear what's going on in your head. *"I'm terrible at math. How can I help my child?"* Here's my answer: Even if you don't understand the math problem itself, you can tell by her explanations whether your child is struggling. If her explanations don't clarify the math for you, you know it's not clear to her either. It's time to set up a meeting with your child's teacher.

Be sure to ask the teacher for a specific plan to boost your child's skills. Ask for weekly progress reports as well. You may not be able to teach your child the math or science, but the timeline will help you uncover the need for assistance before she brings home a failing grade.

Timelines can also help your child remember major plot points in a novel. Purchase a notebook or diary. Label the top of the page with the chapter title or number, and then read a chapter together. (If you prefer, you can read the chapter at different times and summarize together a little later.)

Draw a horizontal line on the notebook page below the chapter title. Go through the chapter a second time together. Each time you identify a major plot point, put a short vertical stroke through the horizontal line and summarize the point in a few brief words beneath it. Each time your child reads a new chapter, ask her to make a new timeline.

For greater retention, have your child skim through all of her previous timelines before reading each new chapter. Come test time, she'll remember much more of the plot. Even more importantly, her ability to retain information in her head will grow and grow. Over time, she'll be able to read increasingly complex texts.

Help your child boil down the chapter into a few main points. These points will jog your child's memory and help her recall what she read. Often, this is a difficult strategy at first. Your child might include many more points on her timeline. Mostly these will be minor details. It's hard at first to sort out the minor details and leave in the main points.

You'll have to have numerous conversations where you guide your child into crossing out the minor details. The more you practice with her, the better she'll get and the more effective her memory will become because she'll learn to focus on the important plot elements.

Rhythm, Rhyme, and Rap

Any time information is turned into a song or rap or is presented with rhyming words, it is easier to remember. Think about it. Which can you remember more easily, the preamble to the Constitution, which you probably learned in junior high, or the lyrics to any ten of your favorite songs from the eighth grade?

My son is constantly surprised when I start singing along with songs on the radio. That's because so many of his songs are remakes of tunes that were popular when I was a teen. Even if I haven't heard them in years, when the radio starts playing my old favorites the lyrics come right back to me.

Suppose you and your child used your creativity to create rhymes, songs, or raps as a way of remembering important information. It's likely that he'll recall that information easily. This is the way the brain works. It picks up information through perceiving patterns. Rhyme and rhythm follow such patterns and make learning easier.

Years ago, when I taught sixth-grade social studies, my students had to learn about one of the first sets of laws in history: Hammurabi's Code. Most of the kids in my class remembered the basics of these laws because we recited this rap:

> Not written on paper; not written on bone,
> They were written on columns made of stone.
> I tell no lies, I tell the truth,
> It's an eye for an eye and a tooth for a tooth,
> Whatever you took, whatever you did,
> You had to make it up; that's the truth now kid.
> So if you stole something small or even grand,
> You'd soon be deprived of your own right hand.
> If you killed with a sword or a club or a knife,
> Hammurabi said you'd pay with your life.

And here's one that you probably know already. Quick! Tell me: When did Columbus arrive in the New World? For many of you, a rhyme has just come to mind:

> In fourteen-hundred-and-ninety-two,
> Columbus sailed the ocean blue.

Never forgot it, did you? Neither will your child. When your child composes raps or songs or rhymes of any kind, don't sweat it if the rhymes aren't perfect. That's not the point of this technique. If he has fun reciting what he wrote, he will remember the factual information contained in his composition. And he'll do it without suffering the tedium of memorizing long lists of information.

Acting/Role-Playing

This is great for remembering historical facts and the major plot elements of a story. In some cases, role-playing can even be used to learn science. The idea is to look at a textbook or your child's notebooks and create a play based on the information you find.

Writing a play about the Selma bus boycott or the plot of *Johnny Tremain* is fun and relatively easy. But you can also turn scientific phenomena into a play. Consider the following vignette:

THE DROPLET: A ONE-ACT DRAMA

Setting: The curtain rises. We are inside an electron microscope at a distinguished university. The voice of Professor Oxbridge, a physicist, can be heard.

Prof. Oxbridge: Today, class, we will see how water is formed. First, let's place an oxygen molecule inside the electron microscope.

Enter: Oxygen Molecule No. 1

Oxygen Molecule No. 1: Where am I? How did I get here? It's so scary in this place, I'm all alone.

An offstage voice can be heard.

Voice: You're not alone. I'm here too!

Enter: Oxygen Molecule No. 2 (the voice)

Oxygen Molecule No. 1: Wow! You look just like me. Are you a relative?

Oxygen Molecule No. 2: I'm not sure. Maybe we're cousins. I've got so many of them I lost count.

Enter: *Hydrogen Molecule*

Oxygen Molecule No. 1: Hey, that guy's not a relative. He doesn't look like us at all.

Oxygen Molecule No. 2: But he seems like a nice guy. Let's ask him to play with us. Hey, dude, do you want to play ring-around-the-rosy?

Hydrogen Molecule: Sure, sounds like fun!

They all hold hands.

Oxygen Molecule No. 1: Hey, something's happening. I can't let go of either of you.

Oxygen Molecule No. 2: I feel funny.

All of the molecules together: I'm changing! We're changing!! We've become one big molecule. Look around; there are more groups just like us. WHAT'S HAPPENING?

Directions: The lights go out for ten seconds. When they go on again, the molecules are gone. In their place is a droplet of water with H_2O painted on its side. The curtain falls.

It's unlikely that your child or anyone participating in this play will forget the formula for water. Writing the play will deepen her memory. This technique can be used for many different topics. For most children, writing and performing skits is fun as well as educational.

Mnemonic Devices

Mnemonic devices are linguistic tricks that aid memory. The famous Columbus couplet, quoted earlier, is an example.

There are quite a few classic mnemonic devices. I will share some with you, but you and your child can also invent your own. The combination of personal creativity and linguistic memory-joggers is very powerful. Take advantage of it. Here are some of the classics:

The original nine planets: *My very educated mother just served us nine pickles.*

(Mercury, Venus, Earth, Mars, Jupiter, Saturn, Uranus, Neptune, Pluto)

Or: *Mary's violet eyes make John sit up nights pining.*

The eight remaining planets: Some of you might be aware that astronomers have downgraded Pluto, which is no longer considered a planet. So now we have:

My very educated mother just served us nuts (or nougats or nachos).

Or: *Mary's violet eyes make John sit up nights.*

Where to place the letter "i": *"i" before "e" except after "C" or when sounding like "ay" as in "neighbor" or "weigh"*

Navigation at sea (and forecasting storms in general):

Red sky at night: sailors' delight;
Red sky in the morning: sailors take warning!

The number of days in a month:

Thirty days has September, April, June, and November;
All the rest have thirty-one,
Except for that contrary

February,
Which has twenty-eight
Most of the time
But in Leap Year twenty-nine.

Nursery Rhymes

Reciting poetry of any kind can build memory. One of the easiest ways to begin is with classic nursery rhymes. Buy a book of children's nursery rhymes or use some of the ones provided below. Do not ask your child to sit down and memorize them. Again, we want this to remain fun. Most children will fall in love with nursery rhymes. Recite these and any others you know, and see which ones your child likes best. Then, for fun, recite the rhyme together at every opportunity. Your child will often lead the way, asking to recite the rhyme over and over again. This is a natural instinct. It builds understanding of the rules of language and it naturally develops memory.

Baa baa Black Sheep, have you any wool?
Yes sir, yes sir, three bags full.
One for my master, one for my dame,
And one for the little boy
Who lives down the lane.
Baa Baa Black Sheep, have you any wool?
Yes sir, yes sir, three bags full.

Diddle, diddle, dumpling, my son John,
Went to bed with his trousers on;
One shoe off, and one shoe on,
Diddle, diddle, dumpling, my son John.

Georgie Porgie pudding and pie,
Kissed the girls and made them cry.
When the boys came out to play,
Georgie Porgie ran away.

Hark hark the dogs do bark
The beggars are coming to town,
Some in rags and some in tags
And one in a velvet gown.

Hey diddle diddle, the cat and the fiddle,
The cow jumped over the moon.
The little dog laughed to see such fun
And the dish ran away with the spoon.

Hickory dickory dock,
The mouse ran up the clock.
The clock struck one,
The mouse ran down,
Hickory dickory dock.

Hot cross buns! Hot cross buns!
One a penny two a penny!
Hot cross buns!
If you have no daughters, give them to your sons.
One a penny two a penny!
Hot cross buns!

Humpty Dumpty sat on a wall.
Humpty Dumpty had a great fall.
All the King's horses, and all the King's men,
Couldn't put Humpty together again.

The itsy-bitsy spider climbed up the water spout.
Down came the rain and washed the spider out.
Out came the sun and dried up all the rain,
And the itsy-bitsy spider climbed up the spout again.

Jack and Jill went up the hill to fetch a pail of water.
Jack fell down and broke his crown,
And Jill came tumbling after.

Jack be nimble;
Jack be quick
Jack jump over
The candlestick.

Jack Sprat could eat no fat;
His wife could eat no lean.
And so between the two of them,
They licked the platter clean.

Little Bo Peep has lost her sheep,
And can't tell where to find them.
Leave them alone and they'll come home,
Bringing their tails behind them.

Little Boy Blue, come blow your horn,
The sheep's in the meadow the cow's in the corn.
But where is the boy who looks after the sheep?
He's under a haystack fast asleep!

Little Miss Muffet sat on her tuffet,
Eating her curds and whey.
Along came a spider,
Who sat down beside her,
And frightened Miss Muffet away!

Little Robin Red Breast sat upon a tree,
Up went Pussy Cat and down went he.
Down came pussy and away Robin ran.
Said little Robin Red Breast, "Catch me if you can!"
Little Robin Red Breast jumped upon a wall,
Pussy Cat jumped after him and almost had a fall;
Little Robin chirped and sang, and what did Pussy say?
Pussy Cat said, "Meeow!" and Robin jumped away.

Old King Cole was a merry old soul,
And a merry old soul was he.
He called for his pipe in the middle of the night,
And he called for his fiddlers three.
Every fiddler had a fine fiddle,
And a very fine fiddle had he.
Oh there's none so rare as can compare,
With King Cole and his fiddlers three.

Old Mother Hubbard
Went to the cupboard
To get her poor doggie a bone;
But when she got there
The cupboard was bare
And so the poor doggie had none.

Pease porridge hot; pease porridge cold,
Pease pudding in the pot, nine days old.
Some like it hot, some like it cold,
Some like it in the pot nine days old.

Pat a cake, pat a cake, baker's man,
Bake me a cake as fast as you can.
Pat it and prick it and mark it with a B,
Then put it in the oven for baby and me.

Peter Peter pumpkin eater,
Had a wife and couldn't keep her.
He put her in a pumpkin shell,
And there he kept her very well.

Polly put the kettle on,
Polly put the kettle on,
Polly put the kettle on,

We'll all have tea.
Sukey take it off again,
Sukey take it off again,
Sukey take it off again,
They've all gone away.

"Pussycat pussycat, where have you been?"
"I've been up to London to visit the Queen."
"Pussycat pussycat, what did you dare?"
"I frightened a little mouse under her chair!"

Rock-a-bye baby on the tree top,
When the wind blows the cradle will rock.
When the bough breaks the cradle will fall,
And down will come baby, cradle and all.

Seesaw Margery Daw,
Johnny shall have a new master.
He shall earn but a penny a day,
Because he can't work any faster.

Simple Simon met a pie man going to the fair.
Said Simple Simon to the pie man, "Let me taste your ware."
Said the pie man to Simple Simon, "Show me first your penny."
Said Simple Simon to the pie man, "Sir, I haven't any!"

Sing a song of sixpence a pocket full of rye,
Four and twenty blackbirds baked in a pie.
When the pie was opened the birds began to sing.
Now wasn't that a dainty dish to set before the king?
The king was in his counting house counting all his money,
The queen was in the parlor eating bread and honey,
The maid was in the garden hanging out the clothes,
When down came a blackbird and bit off her nose!
Starlight star bright,
First star I see tonight:

I wish I may, I wish I might,
Have the wish I wish tonight!

There was a crooked man who walked a crooked mile,
He found a crooked sixpence upon a crooked stile.
He bought a crooked cat that caught a crooked mouse.
And they all lived together in a little crooked house.

Three blind mice, three blind mice,
See how they run, see how they run.
They all ran after the farmer's wife,
Who cut off their tails with a carving knife.
Did you ever see such a thing in your life,
As three blind mice?

This little piggy went to market,
This little piggy stayed at home,
This little piggy had roast beef,
This little piggy had none.
And this little piggy cried "wee wee wee" all the way home!

Twinkle twinkle little star, how I wonder what you are?
Up above the world so high, like a diamond in the sky.
Twinkle twinkle little star, how I wonder what you are?

Wee Willie Winkie runs through the town,
Upstairs and downstairs in his nightgown,
Tapping at the window and crying through the lock,
"Are all the children in their beds? It's past eight o'clock!"

CHAPTER 8

Study Skills

We often tell kids that the way to succeed is to study, study, study! But unless we teach them how, our children often stare at their class notes not understanding why none of the information sticks in their brains. The answer is that the brain works best when information is organized into meaningful patterns. If your child has trouble retaining facts and ideas, it's likely that he hasn't learned to organize ideas mentally.

One great way to achieve organized thinking is to begin visually. This can be done through graphic organizers. A graphic organizer is a visual device to help a child organize his thinking or to understand the way a textbook or article has organized information.

In Chapter 1, you saw some examples of graphic organizers that can help during reading. Following are some additional organizers that can help your child study and review information.

Summary Method

The Summary Method is great for taking notes when your child's teacher is talking, or for focusing on key issues when reading social studies texts and nonfiction articles. This format was designed for college students but it can be used for children in the upper elementary grades and beyond.

It's also a great device for doing research reports. Teachers often complain that students plagiarize when they do reports, copying encyclopedia entries verbatim. When a child learns to use the Summary method, the final product is in his own words. The final summaries are great review materials.

The idea behind the Summary method is to record important information in the Notes section. Then the child boils the notes down to bulleted points and adds them into the Main Ideas column. The final step is to cover up the notes and convert the bulleted points into a summarizing paragraph—the summary. The information has now been recorded in the child's own words.

The child can review using the Summary Method. Since it's in his own language, he'll be more likely to retain the information. An alternative to writing the summary is to use the bulleted points to orally summarize the information for you or anyone who's willing to listen.

Below is an example of the Summary method. I have summarized the cycle of precipitation, a common subject in grade-school and junior-high science classes.

Main Ideas	Notes
Warm water evaporates	Many sources of water on ground—lakes, rivers, oceans, ponds. As weather grows warm, water evaporates and rises into the air. Water molecules cluster together—form clouds. When clouds are heavy enough they release water. If temperature is warm it becomes rain or dew. If temperature is cold it becomes snow, sleet, hail, or ice. Might even form frost on surfaces. As temperature rises again, more water enters the air and cycle starts again.
Rises	
Forms clouds	
Comes down as rain, snow, and so on	
Cycle begins again	

Summary

When warm water evaporates, it rises and forms clouds. Later, the clouds return to the ground as rain in warm weather and snow in cold weather. When the air warms up, the cycle starts again.

Flow Chart

Flow charts are great for having children understand effects and their causes. Notice that I didn't use the more typical term: causes and effects. In my experience, children are often confused when asked to identify causes and effects. The thinking process becomes clearer to them if you begin with the end product: the effect.

In other words: *What happened?* Once that's decided, your child can ask: *What made it happen?*

Let's return to the subject of precipitation. Your child has learned the information recorded in the Summary notes above. Your child has learned the basic facts. Now the teacher asks a review question for an upcoming test. *What causes rain?* Train your child that whenever he's asked about cause, he should jot down a flow chart in a convenient space in his notebook. Remind him that he should always begin with the effect.

In this case the effect is easy to identify: rain. Now, all your child has to do is backtrack and record all of the events leading up to rain.

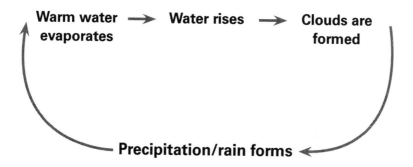

In-Web

This is just another way to record effects and their causes. The circle in the middle shows the effect. Again: rain. The causes are written along the arrows, which are pointing inward toward the effect.

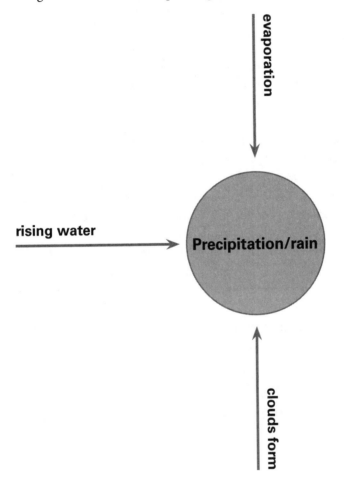

Out-Web

An out-web looks like the in-web but the arrows point outward. This is the one time where you want to write the cause first. The reason? This is a cause with multiple effects. Your child is now considering rain as a cause. The effects are those occurrences that are caused by rain, such as new bodies of water being formed, erosion, or floods.

Shorthand

When your child is taking notes, the goal is for her to do it quickly and efficiently. In Chapter 3, you read about Internet shorthand. Unless the teacher objects, encourage your child to use these when taking notes if she is proficient in it. Make sure your child understands that shorthand must be converted to conventional English when writing reports and essays or when taking tests.

For maximum retention, the notes should be rewritten in standard English the same night. Studying should happen right after a subject has been learned and notes should be reviewed on the weekend.

Cramming on the night before the test is the least effective way to study. Studying that happens briefly but frequently as your child learns a new subject is the best path to retention. Then, the night before the test, a half-hour of review should be sufficient.

The morning of the test, your child might want to spend ten minutes reviewing her original shorthand notes as a memory jogger, but don't overdo it. Too much stress before a test will interfere with her ability to recall facts.

Spattered Vocabulary

The Spattered Vocabulary technique is often used as a pre-reading strategy. However, if children are pressed into writing sentences with unfamiliar vocabulary words, the exercise will be confusing and pointless. What's really being learned?

You may find, however, that the Spattered Vocabulary technique works well as a *review* method. It helps children relearn important words and concepts on a particular topic and remember them better.

The words are placed on a piece of writing paper or on a chart. They will look like bits of paint that you've spattered onto the paper. They will be placed on the page in every direction imaginable. The goal here is to have your child include all the words in a comprehensible paragraph. By spattering them freely on the paper, there's no specific order to the words. Your child will have to do the organizing mentally which builds both memory and comprehension. It doesn't matter if he uses each word in its own sentence or includes several words in a single sentence. There's no specific sentence order required. The only thing that's important is that your child can demonstrate knowledge of the topic. If he can—great! If he can't, then it's time to review.

Project-Planning Calendar

I once got an "emergency" phone call from my son Kenny at 4:30 on a Sunday afternoon. I was in the car on my way to the supermarket to pick up a few groceries. The cell phone rang.

"Dad, I just remembered, I need a poster board and some markers. I have a project that's due tomorrow." *Tomorrow?* I reversed the car and went in the opposite direction as fast as the law would allow. I made it to my local office supply store with ten minutes to spare.

Kenny and I finished the project and he got a good grade. I, on the other hand, was miserable all through the next day. We didn't finish the project until nearly midnight and I don't function well without a good night's sleep. Many of you have had similar experiences, I'm sure.

I made two mistakes. It has always been my habit to review Kenny's homework assignments. But I neglected to ask about long-term projects. I also neglected to ask Kenny to break down his projects into shorter tasks.

Here's what you can do to avoid my mistakes. Get a calendar just for your child. Make it a large calendar that can be hung on the wall. Make sure the calendar has large boxes for handwritten notations.

When your child is given a project or report to do, record the due date on the calendar in red ink. Together, you and your child will then record the different steps that must be taken to complete the project. Every day, check the calendar together to see which part of the project must be done.

Once the project is completed, ask your child to cross it off the calendar. Your goal is to complete the project forty-eight hours before it is due. Display it prominently and proudly in your home before your child hands it in. This will build organizational skills and foster pride of accomplishment.

CHAPTER 9

Writing Builds Better Readers

Literacy is a two-way street. Reading well improves writing and writing well improves reading. Young writers learn the conventions of printed literature and this in turn will lead to greater comprehension when they encounter those conventions in books. When a young writer can use literary conventions to convey her own unique ideas, she has begun to master the English language. This is a major step on the road to becoming a literate adult.

Early Writing

Learning to write well also helps children learn to read and think well. Reading is, among other things, the art of interpreting an author's thoughts. And writing, of course, is the physical extension of one's thoughts. It's thinking on paper.

In first grade, and sometimes in kindergarten, children begin to write. Mostly, they tell personal narratives. At this age, their narratives will be quite simple and will reflect the recent past (yesterday, or last week at the farthest).

You can't expect a six-year-old to tell her experiences of last Christmas because she won't remember most of the details. You can't ask her to invent a story because she doesn't yet have the life experiences to do so. But she can say a lot about the recent events in her world, and she can learn the conventions of print while doing so.

When teaching your child how to write, begin by looking at picture books. Show her how authors tell the events in order. Show her how the pictures match what the words say. And begin to show her simple words. Below, you will find lists of words that children must know at various points in their lives. The first list is for the earliest readers.

The best way to use these lists is to post them on the walls of your home. Begin by posting the letters of the alphabet in order around the room where your child will do writing.

Once you've attached your alphabet line to the walls, place some words from my list under the appropriate letter. You can also add words that your child encounters repeatedly in some of her books. When she writes, she can find these words and copy them into her stories. Don't worry about how she spells the other, less familiar words she uses. If she doesn't know how to spell a lot of words other than those on the wall, allow her to write the first letter of an unfamiliar word and use it as a label over a picture.

Don't put more than ten words on the wall. After your child becomes comfortable writing these words, you can add two or three more. Again, don't add others until your child regularly uses the new words.

Before the actual writing begins, have your child orally retell stories from daily life, such as our trip to the grocery store or our visit to grandma. Many pre-kindergarteners can do this, even before they're ready to write. Guess what? They're learning the conventions of literature even before they've begun putting words to paper. They're learning that narratives are told in order. They're learning that authors (including themselves) stick with an idea and follow it through.

Have your child draw pictures to show a recent event. At first, she can label the pictures with initial letters and make a beginning attempt to copy the words from the wall (they're up there, right?). You can write the story for her on the lines. After a while, encourage her to do her own writing.

This is a common technique used by kindergarten teachers. Children draw images in a large box on a piece of paper. These pictures represent the people, places, and things in the story they're telling. Below are just a few lines on which they can begin the attempt to write sentences. As children grow more proficient, the box gets smaller to make way for a greater number of lines below. This enables the child to write more sentences on a topic than she previously wrote. In these longer stories, she can add in descriptive details rather than just describing the bare-bones events she described in her earlier, shorter writings.

In time, your child can practice continuing her story on additional lined pages. Show her how the authors of her favorite picture books continue the story from one page to the next. At first, she can continue drawing and labeling pictures.

At the same time encourage her to try creating pictures through language. You can do this by encouraging your child to create mental videos. After she writes a story (for example, about a trip to the park), ask her to close her eyes and imagine she's there again. Ask her to name all of the sights, sounds, smells, and feelings she experienced.

You may have to demonstrate or ask leading questions—"What did the poodle look like?" or "How did you feel when the squirrel came down the side of the tree and grabbed the nut you tossed on the grass?"

Your child will then write a second version of the story, adding in all of these details. In time, she will develop the habit of naming details without having to be reminded. Her career as a proficient writer (and reader) has begun.

Writing in the Upper Elementary Grades and Beyond

Older children and young adults can learn more-sophisticated writing techniques to make their work more interesting. Again, as they learn to write well, they will develop greater reading proficiency by practicing the conventions they'll encounter in books. Following are some strategies that older children should practice.

Adding Text Features

If your child is writing a report or research paper, encourage him to break up the text with subsections. Make sure that he sticks to the point of each section. Together, you can examine textbooks, encyclopedias, and articles to see how authors divide up their writing. Looking at samples of other writers' work is always instructive.

Your child can also add illustrations with captions where needed, and fit in charts and maps that clarify information he's included in the main text. If he can use these text features in his writing, he will understand them when he encounters them in his reading.

Introductions

Your child will need to know how writers grab their readers' attention by provoking thought or creating an emotional response. This often begins with the introduction. There are a variety of techniques that writers use when writing introductions. Four of the most popular are:

- Anecdotes
- Provocative statements
- Reflective questions
- Fascinating statistics

Anecdotes

These are short tales of an individual that bring to life the topic the author will discuss. They can be funny or dramatic, even horrific, as long as they grab the attention. Anecdotes can be personal (about an incident in the author's life), or can tell someone else's story. They can be as short as a sentence or two, or they can be one or two paragraphs in length, but no longer.

On May 21, 2006, Anthony deMasters wrapped his car around a light pole and died in a flaming explosion. His girlfriend, Sheila Young, and her sister Emily also died in the flames. Rob Flanders, who was riding shotgun, was tossed from the car and escaped with three broken ribs and a shattered femur. It took him months of physical therapy to recover. All four teens had been drinking heavily that night. Unfortunately, this kind of tragedy happens every day. Teen drinking occurs across America and many teens suffer disastrous consequences when they mix drinking and driving. The problem of teen drinking is widespread throughout the United States.

Provocative Statements

These are brief attention-getting statements. Sometimes these statements can seem illogical until followed by an explanation. Curiosity sucks the reader into the topic.

"Never, ever *tell your students your classroom rules,"* says educational expert Dr. Hal Lanse. "How will they learn?" one teacher asked. Thus began the first day of Lanse's three-day seminar on classroom management. "Youngsters never learn rules by being told about them," Lanse replied. "The rules must be *taught* and role-played. This is the only way that many students will internalize your class rules. This is today's first lesson in behavior management. Let's begin."

Reflective Questions

These are provocative issues raised in question form. They challenge the reader to think about his feelings or opinions before the author shares her thoughts on the subject.

Suppose your best friend since kindergarten tells you that he's gay and that he was born that way; how would you respond?

Fascinating Statistics

This strategy is not unlike sharing an anecdote. The author provides a brief but captivating look into the topic at hand by providing illustrative statistics.

By the next century, less than 5 percent of the world's population will be blond. Golden hair is being bred out of the human population. Genetics, the science that studies changes in the traits we inherit, can help us predict changes that will happen to future generations.

Dialogue and Inner Thought

Writers let us know how characters think by letting them talk. When characters talk, we set off their words with quotation marks. You and your child can examine some of her favorite books and stories to see how quotation marks are used to indicate dialogue. When she writes her own story or interviews somebody for a report, encourage her to include direct speech with quotation marks.

"This bowl of porridge is way too hot," Goldilocks said. "And that one is too cold."

Authors also let us see inside the heads of some of their characters. Most often, direct thought is indicated with italics. Alternatively, some authors use quotation marks. With your child, look for direct thought in some of her favorite chapter books. Encourage her to try the same technique in her own stories. Teachers generally require underlining. Many students can't write neatly enough to show a difference between slanty and non-slanty handwriting.

Mary looked proudly at her daughter, who was writing her own story. *I can't believe it,* Mary thought. *Charlene is a genius!*

Bulleted Points

Our children's lives are filled with standardized tests and that's not going to change anytime soon. Many of the essay questions on these tests are composed of bulleted points. In my career, I've seen hundreds of children get low scores on essays because they fail to address all of the bullets.

One reason is that tests are timed and students feel pressured to "get through" them. I've heard many teachers tell students to take their time and read carefully. And I've heard the same teachers, often in the same lesson, tell their students to push themselves to complete the test on time.

Testing days are pressure cookers for students and teachers alike. Under such high-stakes and high-anxiety conditions, it's no surprise that bright students often screw up by missing some bulleted points on essays.

The more training and practice our children get with bullets, the better they'll function on high-stakes tests. One way to build up their skills is called the "double touch." When your child brings home practice essays, have her write her answer and then reread it. As she rereads have her touch the first bullet in the question and silently read that bulleted point to herself. Then ask her to touch the place in her essay where she addressed that point. Have her repeat the process for every bulleted point on the essay.

Pressure can cause even the best and brightest to forget to address a point. Practicing the "double touch" will help your child build the habit of noticing everything in an essay question that needs to be addressed.

Writing can reinforce her understanding of bulleted points. Earlier in this chapter, you read about types of introductions. Using bulleted points is another approach that your child should try from time to time. When she introduces a new topic, ask her to add in bullets stating all of the subtopics she plans to address.

As I talk about the ancient Egyptians, I will discuss their:

- religion
- architecture
- clothing
- writing system

Academic Vocabulary

As mentioned above, this chapter provides lists of vocabulary words for all age groups. These lists can be used in several ways. You've already learned about posting words on your walls so that your child can check his spelling every time he writes. This technique is not just for our youngest readers. All children, up to and including high schoolers, can use this technique for learning proper spelling

The words included on my lists are not just any words. They're called *academic vocabulary* because these are many of the words that appear over and over on standardized tests, in textbooks, and in articles. Your child is likely to encounter many if not all of these words in his reading, so he should learn to use them in his writing as well.

Whenever possible, include these words in your conversations with your child. It's vital that he hears these words often and uses them in writing, because only through use and repetition will these words become a natural part of his vocabulary. Try asking him to memorize the list and you'll get the same results as generations of educators. He'll learn the words when you're testing him on them, then forget most (if not all) of them a week later.

Memorizing a list doesn't activate the memory. Ongoing encounters with words through writing, reading, and talking is the way. Consciously introduce your older child to some of the new words. As in the case of younger children, introduce ten at first and only a few more as the first group becomes familiar. Three to five new words at a time is sufficient for older children.

GRADES 1–2:

Abbreviation:
The short way of writing a word.

Above:
Over the person, place, or thing you're talking about.

Alphabet:
All the letters in English that we use to form words.

Antonym:
A word that means the opposite of another word.

Author:
The person who wrote a book.

Behind:
Farther back than the person, place, or thing you're talking about.

Below:
Farther down than the person, place, or thing you're talking about.

Biography:
The story of a person's life.

Book:
Pieces of paper with writing on them that are fastened together.

Brother:
The son of the same parents as the person you're talking about.

Calendar:
A chart of all the dates and months of the year.

Capitals:
The big letters used at the beginning of sentences and at the beginning of proper names.

Caption:
The words or title over or under an illustration.

Circle:
Something that is shaped like a ring.

Clock:
A tool that tells us what time it is.

Compare:
To show how things are like each other.

Conclusion:
The ending of a book or story.

Cover:
The front and back of a book.

Date:
The day of the month.

Day:
When the sun is up.

Dictionary:
A book that tells the meanings of words. The words are listed in alphabetical order.

Different:
Not like the person, place, or thing you're talking about.

Fact:
Something that is true.

Family:
A group of people who are related to each other.

Father:
A parent who is a man.

Flag:
A piece of cloth attached to a wooden pole. A flag is often used to stand for something else, like a country or a city.

Glossary:
A type of dictionary that is usually found at the back of a book.

Home:
The place where a person or family lives.

House:
A small building that people live in.

Illustration:
A picture or drawing that shows what an author is talking about.

Illustrator:
The person who draws or paints the pictures in a book.

Index:
An alphabetical list at the back of a book that tells you where in the book to find information.

Label:
A tag or sticker that gives you the name of an object or tells you something about the object.

Letter:
A picture or shape that stands for a sound in the English language.

Month:
One of the twelve parts of the year.

Mother:
A parent who is a woman.

Narrator:
The person who tells the tale in a story or book.

On:
Touching the top of the person, place, or thing you're talking about.

Opinion:
What you think or believe about something.

Over:
Above but not touching the person, place, or thing you're talking about.

Paragraph:
A group of sentences that are all about the same idea.

Poem:
A piece of writing that has rhymes or beats.

Print:
To put words on paper.

Resource:
Something that is helpful to people.

Retell:
To say a story again in your own words.

Rural:
In the country.

Sister:
The daughter of the same parents as the person you're talking about.

Summarize:
To tell the important information in a story briefly and in your own words.

Synonym:
A word that means the same thing as another word.

Under:
Below or beneath the person, place, or thing you're talking about.

Urban:
In the city.

Weather:
What the air around us is like on any day.

Word:
A group of letters that stand for a person, place, thing, or action.

World:
Our planet and all the people and places on it.

GRADES 3–5

Alliteration:
When two or more words in a sentence or poem begin with the same letter.

Article:
A short piece of nonfiction writing.

Brief:
Short, as when you tell something in the shortest way possible.

Chapter:
One part of a book, in which some of the story or information is told.

Character:
A made-up person in a book.

Conflict:
A disagreement between two characters in a book.

Describe:
To explain what something looks or feels like.

Dialogue:
Speech, as when two or more characters in a story are directly talking to each other.

Encyclopedia:
A book that gives information on many different subjects.

Explain:
To give clear information about the subject you're talking about.

Fiction:
A story that is made up from an author's imagination.

Children should understand that while fictional tales are imaginary, they may contain "truths" (meaning wisdom or insights) about life, but that doesn't make them factual. Kids do have to know the conventional distinction between fact and fiction, if only so they're not marked wrong when they're tested on it (or get fired from their reporter jobs for making up stories that contain truths.

Frequently:
Often; something that happens a lot of the time is said to happen frequently.

Highlight:
To call attention to important information in a story or article by using color.

Identify:
To recognize the person, place, thing, or information you're looking for.

Inquire:
To ask.

Internet:
The world of information that you connect to using a computer.

Moral:
A lesson to be learned from a story.

Motivation:
The thoughts and feelings and inspirations that make a character behave the way they do.

Narrative:
A story that usually has a beginning, middle, and end.

Occur:
To happen.

Optional:
Not required, as when it's your choice to do something or not do it.

Origin:
The beginning or cause of something.

Overview:
A general idea of what's in a book or what's needed to complete a task.

Periodical:
A magazine or newspaper that comes out at regular times.

Plural:
More than one.

Predict:
To guess what might happen next, based on information you have read and thought about.

Primary source:
An object or piece of writing that was created by somebody who lived during the time you're learning about.

Proofread:
To reread your work in order to find mistakes that need correcting.

Prove:
To show facts that make it clear that your opinion is correct.

Purpose:
A reason for doing something.

Reference book:
A book that provides factual information.

Secondary source:
Information about history that is told by somebody who didn't live in that particular time and place.

Singular:
Only one of something.

Text feature:
All of the information in a book that is outside of the main writing but still tells us about what's in the book (titles, captions, illustrations, boxed text, etc.).

Theme:
A main idea carried through a story or book.

Title:
The name of a book or article.

Traits (or character traits):
The parts of a character's personality that are special to that character.

GRADES 6–8

Affect:
To change a person, place, or thing in some way.

Alter:
To create a change in a person, place, or thing.

Anecdote:
A short story that describes just one event.

Annotations:
Notes that are outside the main part of a story or article but that tell more information about the story or article.

Annual:
Taking place once every year.

Anthology:
A collection of stories, poems, or articles that were once published separately.

Anticipate:
To think about something that you know will happen in the future, as when you think about the gifts you'll get on your birthday coming up.

Argument:
Your strong reasons for giving an opinion.

Aspects:
Different sides or parts of a subject.

Assert:
To express your opinion strongly.

Capable:
Able to do something well.

Chronology:
A telling of events in the order that they happened.

Citation:
Information about a reference source used in a book or article.

Coherent:
Well-organized, clear, and easy to follow.

Conceive:
To form an idea in your mind.

Concise:
Something that is expressed briefly and clearly.

Constituents:
The parts out of which something is made.

Contradict:
To disagree with.

Convey:
To express or communicate.

Correspond:
Go along with or be in agreement with.

Credible:
Believable.

Criteria:
A set of rules or guidelines by which something will be judged.

Critique:
To judge the quality of somebody's performance or work.

Crucial:
Of the greatest importance.

Debate:
To defend your opinion against someone else's opinion.

Deduce:
To form an opinion or draw a conclusion after observing the facts.

Defend:
To forcefully present proof in support of your opinion.

Depict:
To describe something in words.

Determine:
To decide what you believe is correct or true.

Differentiate:
To see the differences between two or more things.

Distinguish:
To tell the difference between two or more things.

Document:
To provide written proof (verb); or something written down that provides proof or information (noun).

Editorial:
An article that presents your opinion on a topic.

Effect:
The results of an action or series of actions.

Emphasize:
To strongly call attention to a fact, an idea, or a point of view.

Equivalent:
Something that is equal to or the same in value as something else.

Evaluate:
To judge the worth of something.

Eventual:
Happening sometime in the future.

Evidence:
Proof or facts that show something has happened or is true.

Exaggerate:
To describe something in a way that makes it seem bigger, better, or worse than it actually is.

Excerpt:
Writing that has been taken from a larger book, story, or article.

Explicit:
Clearly stated.

Feasible:
Able to be accomplished.

Figment:
Something that is imagined and not real.

Foreshadow:
In a story, to hint that something will happen before it actually does.

Illegible:
Can't be read because the writing is unclear.

Implicit:
Not directly stated; assumed or understood through indirect clues.

Imply:
To hint something without saying it outright.

Include:
To add in something or someone.

Incorporate:
To make something part of something else.

Indicate:
To point something out.

Induce:
To cause something to happen or to persuade someone to take a particular action.

Influence:
To persuade a person to behave differently or to have sufficient power to change something in the world.

Inform:
To provide with factual information.

Inquire:
To ask or search for information.

Intention:
A person's purpose for doing something.

Interact:
To have contact with another and to have an effect on each other.

Interpret:
To understand and explain the meaning of something.

Introduction:
The beginning of a book, story, article, or report where the topic is announced.

Invariably:
Without ever changing.

Legible:
Written clearly enough to be read.

Objective:
A goal.

Paraphrase:
To restate something in your own words.

Passage:
One part of a longer piece of writing.

Perspective:
A person's point of view.

Plausible:
Believable; likely to be true.

Portray:
To describe in words.

Presume:
To believe something to be true.

Previous:
Earlier than; before.

Prior:
Earlier than; before; synonymous with *previous*.

Propose:
To suggest a course of action.

Refer:
To mention or direct attention to.

Reflect:
To think about.

Relate:
Tell about.

Relationship:
The connection or bond between two things.

Relevant:
Important to a point being discussed.

Significance:
The importance of something.

Speculate:
To guess.

Stance:
Point of view or opinion.

Subsequent:
Next.

Superfluous:
Extra; more than is needed.

Thesis:
A theory or idea about something.

Unique:
One of a kind.

Utilize:
To make use of.

Valid:
Correct; reasonable.

Verify:
To prove; to check the truth about something.

Viewpoint:
Belief or opinion.

HIGH SCHOOL

Allude:
To indirectly refer to someone or something.

Ambiguous:
Unclear; having more than one possible meaning.

Annals:
Records or historical accounts.

Antithesis:
The direct opposite.

Archetype:
The model or most perfect example.

Chronicle:
An account or historical record.

Denote:
To illustrate or refer to.

Euphemism:
A nicer way of saying something; a substitute word or phrase often for a more unpleasant word or phrase.

Fundamental:
Basic or main.

Ideology:
Belief system.

Missive:
A letter or written message.

Novel:
Unique.

Paradox:
A statement that seems to contain contradictions but may nevertheless be true.

Parameters:
Boundaries or limits.

Ponder:
To think over.

Predominant:
The most important or influential.

Principle:
A rule or belief.

Transcend:
To exceed or go beyond.

Vital:
Necessary for life; or very important.

CHAPTER 10

Multiple Intelligence Strategies That Improve **Critical Thinking**

Achieving excellence has been a goal of civilizations throughout history. Be it through sport or intellectual achievement human beings have sought to reach their highest potential. We are a competitive species, too (possibly for survival reasons initially); and we often measure our physical and mental prowess in comparison to others. As early psychologists began to define and measure intelligence, it is no surprise that mental acuity was measured comparatively. Over time, however, the measurement of intelligence has become quite sophisticated. Contemporary notions of intelligence can help adults support children's intellectual growth.

The History and Impact of IQ Reading Tests

In the late 1800s, scientists began studying the human mind to see what makes some individuals higher achievers than others. By the early 1900s, the first measures of (so-called) intelligence began to emerge. The Paris school system grew interested in these assessments, turning to psychologist Alfred Binet to develop a test that would help identify children who needed extra help. With the help of Theodore Simon, Binet developed the first major educational intelligence test, the Binet-Simon Intelligence Test.

Interest spread to the United States, and the state of California turned to Lewis Termin, a Stanford University professor, to customize a test for their schoolchildren. The Stanford-Binet test was born. A revised form of this test is used to this day.

Termin was the first to coin the phrase *intelligence quotient* (IQ). Briefly, the baseline score for one's peer group is 100. This is average. If you test more than ten points below below this score, you're considered below average intelligence. If you test thirty points or more above 100, you're considered above average intelligence.

By World War I, the U.S. military got in on the act. Our armed forces wanted to develop a quick way to assess which recruits could handle intellectually demanding jobs and which were less likely to succeed. The goal was to match a large number of people in the military bureaucracy with suitable jobs and to do so quickly and with relative ease.

As time went on, IQ tests grew in popularity. They were used to match people with appropriate vocations and educational opportunities, which was thought to be a good idea at the time. Then, came the lawsuits.

By the 1970s, when the Civil Rights Movement had expanded people's awareness, IQ tests came into disrepute. The tests, it turned out, were biased. They used linguistic and cultural references that were most familiar to white middle-class people. IQ tests were more a measure of one's background knowledge than the size of one's intellect.

The result: Many people who were denied access to higher-paying jobs began to litigate—successfully. These lawsuits were costly; thus, IQ tests were eliminated by many businesses. Even so, many colleges believed these tests could determine which students were capable of working at the intellectual level the course work demanded.

IQ is based on the idea that we are each born with a fixed intelligence level. Reading tests follow the same model. The people who design and distribute tests believe that students have to fall along the classic bell curve with most falling in the middle and smaller numbers gathered at the extreme ends.

Today, many educators and psychologists believe that the classic view of intelligence is inaccurate. IQ tests do not tell us how smart your child is (or isn't); they tell us how your child is performing at one given moment, that being the hour or so when he takes the test. It is now believed that IQ can be increased through education and through various mental challenges such as puzzles and video games.

And so much can distort the results. Along with cultural biases, nerves, lack of sleep, a poor breakfast, construction noises outside, anything can warp the results of your child's test. This is why the current political trend toward high-stakes testing is unfair. It denies opportunities to many children based on flawed data.

High Stakes Testing Doesn't Provide Good Data

Don't misinterpret this message. Standardized tests often serve as an early warning system for children who need extra help. They should not, however, be used exclusively to screen children out of the next grade.

Only a collection of data, provided across many months—portfolios, class tests, teacher and parent observations, and the like—should be used to determine your child's future. If anyone tells you, based on a single test, that your child isn't bright or that he shouldn't go to the next grade, *view that person as nothing less than your child's personal enemy.*

Challenge them. Don't let them get away with it. And for heaven's sake don't let your child believe the hype. A negative self-image is one of the most destructive forces in the world.

Now for a dirty little secret. Test-makers and many educational leaders won't want you to know this. Test-makers design standardized tests to ensure that the scores will follow the bell curve format. Got it? They make sure that a sizable number of children cannot possibly attain the top scores.

There's a term known to all test-makers: *negative skew*. Before publishing and selling their assessments, test-makers field test them. If too many children do well, this is negative skew. In the eyes of the test-makers and the districts that buy the tests, a preponderance of high scores is considered bad, bad, bad.

So what happens next? The test-makers add in trick questions to force more children toward the middle and lower end of the curve. This is why many literacy experts say that reading tests don't test reading ability. Rather, they test your child's ability to take a reading test. Huh? Let me explain.

The test your child is taking this year has wording that's designed to confuse him. If he gets fooled, what do you know? You know that he can't figure out the tricks. This doesn't mean he's a poor reader. The shocking truth is that the results of reading tests are not predictive of future success.

Equally shocking: If an IQ or reading test is used as an excuse to hold your child back, his chance of becoming a dropout later in life has increased dramatically. The damage can be devastating and lifelong. And for what? For a lie. One test should not become the be-all-and-end-all.

Here's another surprise: High scores on standardized tests are not predictive of future success. Many academic high achievers fail in the job market because they don't have the personal skills that enable them to work collaboratively with others. Those with modest scores and strong interpersonal skills do better.

Why Test?

So why test at all? Well, there are still the lowest achievers. Their scores tell us that there's probably (but not always) a serious problem. A low standardized test score should be used to alert parents and teachers to a possible problem. Further assessments of the types mentioned above should be employed and an individualized educational plan should be developed for your child.

Right now, such plans are legally mandated (and rarely implemented well) for special education students. As parents, we need to insist that our schools develop such plans and monitor our children's progress. If special services are needed, take advantage of them, but be aware that many children who receive extra support can improve without being placed into special education.

The IQ Myth Exploded: Gardner's Theory of Multiple Intelligences

We live today with the results of a checkered history that grew out of the early IQ movement. There is a different way of looking at intelligence, one that was formally presented to the world in 1983 by Harvard professor Howard Gardner. Gardner's research on *multiple intelligences* exploded the IQ myth.

Gardner revealed that intelligence is not a single fixed entity measurable on a mathematical scale. Instead, every person has intellectual skills in a variety of different areas. There are skills that are dominant in some people and weaker in others, but we can always build these up.

The world is not divided into smart people and dumb people. It's divided into people with different strengths. This is why the human race has survived. ***Everyone has some skill that the human race needs.*** We need to find those skills and help our children build them up.

Also, if we train our young readers and thinkers with multiple intelligences in mind, we can help them grow intellectually. Multiple intelligences, since the 1980s, have become very popular among educators. Unfortunately, they're often implemented in ways that prove to be more concerned with entertainment than learning.

I think of the educational expert I once saw who demonstrated how to teach geography while dancing the Macarena. This might get a laugh from some children but I doubt that this will have the biggest impact possible on our children's capacity to learn. I have attended many multiple intelligences workshops over the years but usually walked away with little of substance.

This next section offers a series of useful strategies. You will see that many of these strategies activate several of Gardner's intelligences. Among these are:

- Verbal/linguistic intelligence
- Visual/spatial intelligence
- Bodily/kinesthetic intelligence
- Interpersonal intelligence
- Intrapersonal intelligence

This list is not exhaustive, but the items listed are those included in the learning strategies that I've found most useful. They not only enhance children's thinking capacity, they also build interest in learning. Educational research has told us for decades that *chalk-and-talk*, standing in front of a class lecturing and writing notes, is the least effective way to help children learn. Unfortunately, it's still the most common form of teaching in the United States.

If you engage your child in activities that engage multiple intelligences, you're more likely to hit some that fall in line with his best intellectual tendencies. Such activities will be exciting and he'll be more likely to view learning as enjoyable and desirable. Pleasure is a necessary precursor to learning. You can't force intellectual engagement, but you can invite it. That's where multiple intelligence activities come in.

The Literary or Historical Jigsaw (Ages 7–14)

This strategy is best done with other people—family members or friends. It's therefore an interpersonal activity as well as a visual/spatial activity.

Over time, collect many magazine pictures and postcards. After your child has read a novel or learned about a historical period, have him cut up several of these images. They should represent one scene in the novel or one historical incident. Have another person put them together again and try to identify the event your child has recreated.

This activity will help your child translate his knowledge from a purely linguistic experience to one that is enriched through images. If he's a visual learner, the jigsaw activity will be fun while challenging his communication skills. If others can't figure out what is represented in the puzzle, then ask your child to explain his thinking. This will add a verbal element.

Simon Says (Ages 7–14)

This is a great activity for bodily/kinesthetic learners.

This version of Simon Says is a variation on the popular childhood game. It can help your child learn a great variety of subjects. This example will help teach the concept of nouns and verbs. Each player should have two large pieces of paper or flash cards. One card should say *noun*; the other should say *verb*.

In front of you are cards or large pieces of paper each with a single word on it—a noun or verb, of course. One at a time you hold them up and say, "Simon Says: noun or verb?" Your child and any other participants (get her friends involved if possible) should stand up, hold up the correct sign, and shout *Noun!* or *Verb!*

Each participant who calls out the correct answer continues playing. Anyone who's incorrect must sit down until one person is standing—the winner. If several participants keep winning, then after a while you can call it a draw.

Simon Says can be played with a mind-boggling array of subjects: mammal/fish, red state/blue state, triangle/quadrilateral, and on and on. Have fun choosing topics with your child.

Travel Brochures (Ages 7–18)

Since travel brochures can include maps, charts, and illustrations as well as writing, they're great learning tools for visual/spatial learners as well as verbal/linguistic learners. As your child creates them, display the brochures around your home. Have visitors read and discuss them with your child.

At home, study the brochures you find at travel agencies and see how the images and words are arranged. Then your child can cut up magazines pictures, draw pictures, or download images that reflect the scenes or historical period he's studying in school. Encourage your child to create a brochure that imitates the style of the travel brochures you collected.

Travel brochures should begin with on-the-ground research. Visit travel agencies and collect brochures. If the travel agent isn't too busy, you and your child can inquire about exotic locales and popular attractions. Before you've even begun creating the travelogue, you've already helped your child gain some more of that all-important background knowledge.

At home, study the brochures and see how the images and words are arranged. Then your child can cut up magazine pictures, draw pictures, or download images that reflect the scenes or historical period he's studying in school. Encourage your child to create a brochure that imitates the style of the travel brochures you collected.

This activity will deepen his engagement with the novel or social studies topic and it will help (in a fun way) fix information into his memory. You can even use this activity for science. Your child can create a travelogue of a cell, the human body, the solar system, and so forth.

Graphic Novels (Ages 7–18)

Creating posters and graphic novels can help visual/spatial learners improve their reading comprehension and stamina.

A lot of teachers look down on graphic novels because they're not "good literature" and because they have few words. This is a mistake. Graphic novels are often a necessary first step for children who need to build up their reading stamina. They also contain topics, such as sci-fi and action-adventure, that kids love.

Of course, we don't want our kids to stay with graphic novels alone. In time, hopefully, they will move to more complex works of literature. It's also okay for them to go back and forth between different literary forms: today a novel, tomorrow a graphic novel, next week a memoir, and along the way the latest glossy for tweens or teens.

Experience with graphic novels can be a gold mine. When moving on to more-challenging books or when learning history, your child can create graphic novels that demonstrate her learning. She will be engaged with the compositional and artistic aspects of this activity and will practice communicating information in a coherent, articulate manner.

Writing graphic novels will obligate your child to learn specific text features, such as captions, speech bubbles, and thought bubbles. These also appear in political cartoons, textbooks, and advertisements. Learning to work with these text features will increase your child's comprehension when she encounters them in places beyond graphic novels.

Character and Historical Figure Resumes (Ages 12–18)

This strategy works best for children who already have some liking for verbal/linguistic experiences. It's also evaluative in nature. Your child is required to judge the strong and weak points of a character. This will take him to a deeper comprehension level.

While all the activities in this chapter are interpersonal, requiring good communication skills, this activity is highly intrapersonal. Your child will have to look inside himself and decide his own values as he chooses between the candidates.

The task: Character and historical figure resumes work best as a compare/contrast activity. Your child will write two or more resumes and decide which of the individuals will get an imaginary job. He can compare characters within books and time periods or across books and time periods. In other words, characters within a novel might "compete" for a job, or characters in very different novels can do so. Historical figures from the same era can compete, or characters from different eras can do so.

As an example, there are two resumes below. (You yourself would have to be very creative in putting such resumes together. Enjoy.) The task is to hire one of the historical individuals for a job. In this case, a new educational organization, TRUE (Teaching Real Understanding of Equality), needs a new spokesperson to help advertise their program to high schools across America. The spokesperson will appear on TV ads, in newspaper interviews, and in personal visits to many schools.

Your child must decide which individual should get the job. He must use the specific facts in each resume to verbally justify his decision. It is not your job to guide him to a specific candidate. This is not a right or wrong activity. Your job is to make sure that your child gives clear reasons, based on the information in the resumes, for his decision.

BAYARD RUSTIN

Work History
- Founded the New York chapter of the Congress of Racial Equality.
- Speech writer and organizer for Dr. Martin Luther King. Influenced Dr. King's use of Gandhi's philosophy of nonviolence.

Organizations/Memberships
- Society of Friends (Quakers)
- War Resisters League

Education
- Attended three colleges but did not attain a degree.

Life Challenges
- Jailed for two years as a conscientious objector. Refused to participate in the Vietnam War.
- As an openly gay man, Rustin was pressured by leaders of the Civil Rights Movement to work behind the scenes.

BOBBY SEALE

Work History
- Mechanic for U.S. Air Force.
- Founder (along with Huey P. Newton) of Black Panther Party for Self Defense.
- Organized many anti-poverty programs including the Free Breakfast Program for Children, which was run out of a San Francisco church.
- As members of the Black Panthers, Seale and his compatriots followed the Oakland police around while carrying guns in order to monitor and demonstrate resistance to police brutality.

Organizations/Memberships
- Afro American Association at Merritt College (cofounder)
- Black Panther Party for Self Defense (cofounder)

Education
- Attended Merritt College.

Life Challenges
- Accused of conspiring to incite a riot at the 1968 Democratic National Convention. Sentenced to four years in prison by the judge because of his frequent verbal interruptions of the proceedings.
- Tried for participating in the murder of an alleged FBI informant, with the trial ending in a hung jury.

Literary and Historical Editorials (Ages 12–18)
This activity is verbal/linguistic, interpersonal, and intrapersonal. If you add in technology, it can also become visual/spatial.

Editorials are reasoned opinions. They defend a point of view; therefore, your child will have to know the facts about a character's or historical figure's motivations and actions. She must give a reasoned opinion on a character's response to a scene in a book or an actual historical incident. The editorials in this activity will answer one of two questions: *Did the character or historical figure make the right decision? Did the character or historical figure take the correct action?*

With your child, examine editorials from various newspapers. Choose papers that are at a comfortable level for your child. The most sophisticated young readers may do well with the *New York Times*, but many will find the *Times* way too challenging. Your local daily paper will be better for most children.

Look at the language used by editorial writers to trigger an emotional reaction. Which words and phrases create a negative feeling? Which create a positive feeling? Ask your child to write these on index cards (one card per word or phrase). When writing her editorial, your child can consult her cards and select the language she wants to use to convince her readers that her opinion regarding the character's actions is justifiable.

If you have the time, money, and inclination, you can take this activity a step further. You and your child can examine online and TV editorials. If you have the capacity to produce Web pages or videos, you can teach her to design some of her own. What a delight to share these with relatives, friends, and visitors to your home. Such activities will give your child great confidence.

Historical Dramatics (Ages 7–18)

Many children love to write and perform plays. Writing and performing skits is a joyfully verbal, visual, and interpersonal activity.

You may find that playwriting is better suited to enacting historical episodes than to recreating literary scenes. This is because many chapter books already include dialogue. Children tend to copy an author's dialogue rather than inventing their own. If, however, they're writing about a historical figure, there's rarely any dialogue at hand. More inventiveness is required when children write historical plays.

Choose a historical episode that your child is studying. Ask him to jot down the important figures involved and a brief description of the event. Next, look at plays for young people. Together, you and your child can examine how the plays are written. Look at how stage directions are indicated and how dialogue is placed. (It's different from the way novelists do it.)

Then your child can begin writing. After the play is done, the two of you can perform it with other family members. You can also invite your child's friends to perform with him for your family.

You can even produce videos if you like and screen them for visitors. This is much more exciting than merely posting your child's report card on the refrigerator door.

CHAPTER 11

Boys and Reading: A Very Special Challenge

Often, teachers and parents have way too rigid an idea of what constitutes "good books" and what doesn't. They view some books as intellectual and others as trash. They want to steer kids away from bad books—the books boys like. But if we want boys to become passionate, skilled readers, we have to grab them where they live, or we will fail them.

Educators have recognized for a long time that boys are more resistant to reading and often perform below girls their age on standardized reading tests. Working on the front line with hundreds of teachers and thousands of their students, I have seen greater resistance to reading from boys than from girls. This resistance can manifest itself in ways ranging from dozing in class to blatantly disruptive behavior. (It's my own unscientific theory that the first paper plane was launched during a reading lesson.)

According to statistics posted on the International Reading Association's Web site, 39.9 percent of boys who were surveyed said that reading was boring; 11.1 percent said that the stories they were asked to read were boring; and 7.7 percent complained that they just couldn't get into the stories. Got the picture? Boys can't stand what we ask them to read.

I've heard teachers' complaints for years. "All they want to read is *Goosebumps*." "He won't read the assigned chapters." "I had to take the newspaper away from him; he was reading *that* instead of the assigned chapter." Instead of trying to engage boys, we try to shove books that are developmentally inappropriate down their throats.

We can continue to follow this course and keep scratching our heads when we fail to intimidate boys into reading. Or we can learn about how boys really read—and succeed with them. This is what boys typically like:

- Action-adventure
- Animals
- Anime/graphic novels
- Bad boys and daredevils
- Fantasy/sci-fi
- Gross or potty humor (the success of Captain Underpants was not a fluke)
- Heroes/bully bashers
- Informational books and magazines (on topics of their interest, not yours)
- Male protagonists (many boys won't put up with heroine-driven novels)
- Mystery/suspense
- Social outcasts

Following is a list of books, some popular with teachers and some not, that contain one or more elements from the list above. I have given age ranges for these books, but remember that these are approximate. Children of the same age can read at different levels. Please refer to Chapter 2 to help your child select an appropriate-level book.

Again, never tell him, "This book is too babyish; pick something else." Battering your child's self-esteem won't turn him into a serious reader. Determine his level and areas of interest and start from there. Gradually move him up by level as his comprehension and concentration develop. My ongoing and most important message is: Make sure he's enjoying what he reads.

Informational books and magazines are often read socially. Ever seen boys collect baseball cards? They gather in packs and study the information on the cards as a group. They do the same with informational books and magazines. I recommend that you buy lots of magazines for your child to keep in his room, and others to produce as new offerings when your child has other boys visiting. Watch them go to town over the magazines.

You don't have to worry about the level of magazines, by the way. Even if your child can't read all the articles, there will be short pieces, statistics, and intriguing facts that will still capture his attention. So pick up those motorcycle and wrestling and outdoor sports magazines. This is reading, too!

A note on series: If possible, when buying or borrowing a series, get all the books. Many children find it annoying to begin with the third or tenth book in a series; and it's even more annoying to get into a book and not have the very next episode. There's a comprehension issue here, too. Often you have to read the earliest books in the series to fully understand plot developments and character relationships.

BOOKS FOR THE EARLY ELEMENTARY GRADES (K–3)

Arnold, Tedd. *Parts*

For the "gross-me-out" set, this is the tale of a boy who thinks he's falling apart. Is that wet stuff coming out of his nose really part of his brain? And is that bellybutton lint or are his insides falling out?

Buehner, Caralyn and Mark Buehner, illustrator. *Superdog: The Heart of a Hero*

He's a hot dog *and* a hero. Dexter, the downtrodden dachshund, starts working out in an effort to release his inner Rin Tin Tin.

Cronin, Doreen and Harry Bliss, illustrator. *Diary of a Worm*

This is the diary of a baseball-capped worm who tells of his daily activities.

DiTerlizzi, Tony. *Ted*

Ted, a bizarre dog-eared creature, has been banned from the house. Imaginary friends are not allowed inside, you see. That is, until Ted reveals a secret: he's a second-generation imaginary friend, having once palled around with the hero's harried father.

Donaldson, Julia and Axel Scheffler, illustrator.
The Gruffalo

Talk about the mouse that roared! The tiny hero of this book scares off predators by inventing a horrible beast, the Gruffalo. But the Gruffalo turns out to be real and he too wants mouse meat to munch on. The clever mouse fools the Gruffalo by convincing him that all the other creatures are running because he, the mouse, is a Gruffalo-eating carnivore.

Dr. Seuss

The Cat in the Hat. Perhaps the most lovable anarchist in history, this cat leads two bored children into a mess of trouble. The results are good, disorderly fun.

How the Grinch Stole Christmas. Dr. Seuss's lovable villain does his best to steal Christmas from all of Whoville, only to discover that the true spirit of Christmas lies in the heart and not in the tinsel. The message of this classic is as relevant today as it ever was.

Gibbons, Gail

If I ran the U.S. Treasury, I would pay out enough money to buy every American child a copy of each of Gail Gibbons's books. Gibbons is popular with boys, girls, and teachers. Her beautifully illustrated nonfiction books cover a wide array of topics, and the list is still growing. If you want to expose your child to a vast array of facts and vocabulary, give him as many of Gibbons's books as you can. To build on this knowledge base, visit museums, businesses, zoos, or any place where you can interact live with the worlds described in this prolific author's nonfiction. For a list of her books you can visit her Web site at *www.gailgibbons.com.*

Gould, Robert. *Big Stuff* series

These picture books are about the types of machines, such as monster trucks and earth movers, that little boys find interesting.

Goodman, Susan E. and Elwood H. Smith, illustrator.
The Truth About Poop

No, this is not a book about potty training. It's a funny, honest informational book about human and animal excrement. It's chock full of scientific (if gross) facts. With this book, Goodman has established herself as the leading "stool pigeon" of children's literature.

London, Jonathan and Frank Remkiewicz, illustrator.
Froggy Gets Dressed

Froggy doesn't want to hibernate in winter like frogs are supposed to. When he tries to go out, his mother insists he wrap himself in all sorts of outerwear. Will Froggy go out and play or will the battle over clothing wear down his high-risk behavior?

Martin, David and Frank Remkiewicz, illustrator. *Piggy and Dad Go Fishing*

Too many dads would put down a child like Piggy. Piggy's father, however, is an enlightened creature. On a fishing trip, Piggy cannot stand the idea of skewering the worm or killing the fish. He and Dad start a new sport, one in which violence against other living creatures is not part of the mix. This book is a great tool for fathers who wish to engage their sons in non-judgmental ethical conversations at the very earliest of ages.

McMullan, Kate and Jim McMullan, illustrator. *I Stink!*

The title is a declaration of pride. The hero is a garbage truck. This is his life story. When boys get near this book, with its cheeky illustrations, they'll smell a winner.

Monsell, Mary Elise and Lynn Munsinger, illustrator.
Underwear!

A zebra and an orangutan, both avid fans of underwear couture, attempt to cheer up a grouchy buffalo with "underwear" humor.

Osborne, Mary Pope and Sal Murdocca, illustrator. The *Magic Tree House* series

These are great books for getting children interested in all sorts of topics. They're fictional stories, but you can follow up by learning more with your child in other books or online. In this series, siblings Jack and Annie find a tree house with a magical library inside. The books transport them to many different times and places. Be forewarned: The books are meant to be read in sets of four. Each book in a set contains clues or challenges that help Jack and Annie solve a mystery.

Pilkey, Dav. *Dogzilla*

The smell of barbecue sauce awakens the dreaded Dogzilla. Can the citizens of Mousopolis stop her and escape the ravages of her killer breath?

Rylant, Cynthia, Suçie Stevenson (occasional coauthor), and Carolyn Bracken, illustrator. *Henry and Mudge* series

Henry has no friends and no brothers or sisters. No other kids live on his block. So Mom and Dad give him Mudge, an affable, oversized pooch. This likable series follows the archetypal boy and his dog through a series of gently comic adventures.

Scieszka, Jon and Lane Smith, illustrator

The Stinky Cheese Man and Other Fairly Stupid Tales. These gross, irreverent send-ups of traditional fairy tales will have boys snickering with mischievous delight. One caution: Readers will miss the point of this book if you haven't first exposed them to the original fairy tales.

The True Story of the Three Little Pigs. We all know the story of the Three Little Pigs. Or do we? Alexander T. Wolf (yes, that Wolf), now imprisoned for his crimes, tells his version of the tale. Wolf claims he was framed. If you want to get very young children using their critical faculties, ask them to judge the honesty of Wolf's claims.

Sendak, Maurice. *Where the Wild Things Are*

Mischievous Max, dressed as a wolf, has been sent to bed without supper. But a jungle, wild and beautifully illustrated, springs up in Max's room, allowing him to continue his adventures.

Shannon, David. *No, David!*

With illustrations of a child who is at once revolting and lovable, this is the story of a boy whose impulsiveness gets him into trouble time and again.

Slangerup, Erik John and John Manders, illustrator. *Dirt Boy*

Fister (yes, that's the hero's name) has run away from a fate worse than death—his bath. Out in the woods he meets a decidedly unwashed giant. The two share the joys of getting shamelessly, gleefully, disgustingly dirty. This story has a tragic ending. Fister returns home and his Mom, with the aid of a hose and countless bars of soap, cleans him up. But oh, what fun he had living the life of an antihero right up to the bitter, antibacterial end.

Van Allsburg, Chris. *Jumanji*

A board game becomes a living nightmare from which the characters must escape.

Warner, Gertrude Chandler and various illustrators. *The Boxcar Children* series

The four Alden siblings, recently orphaned, run away from their grandfather, whom they mistakenly believe to be mean and unloving. The children wind up living in a boxcar. Subsequent books in the series find the children reunited with their grandfather but still encountering adventure after adventure. While the tales are a bit old-fashioned (they were written in the 1940s), they're great books for one special reason—Warner's stories are interwoven with the 500 most commonly used words in the English language. What an easy and delightful way to learn vocabulary! (Note: There are more than a hundred titles in the series, and not all were written by Warner in her lifetime. The rest have been written by contemporary authors; while entertaining, these cannot guarantee the same level of vocabulary enrichment provided by the originals.)

Wiesner, David

Sector 7. One parent's troublemaker is another parent's revolutionary. In this wordless adventure story, a boy meets a cloud on top of the Empire State Building. They run away to Sector 7, a cloud factory, where the boy helps the clouds rearrange themselves into all sorts of fun shapes. The adults in the story hate this act of rebellion, but children will love the way Manhattan's skyline is transformed into a panorama of cloudy cutouts.

Tuesday. They're green, they can fly, and they're mischievous. For one raucous night, Wiesner unleashes a pack of rascally frogs that travel on antigravity lily pads causing harmless havoc in a sleepy town. Like *Sector 7*, this book is nearly wordless.

Wiles, Deborah and Jerome Lagarrigue, illustrator. *Freedom Summer*

Narrator Joe and his best pal John Henry discover in 1964 that the passage of the Civil Rights Act does not mean the end of racism. In an act of consummate ugliness, the local town fills the public swimming pool with tar rather than permit it to be integrated. Joe and John Henry exemplify the saying that "a child shall lead us" as they end the book with an act of defiance that is filled with the transcendent beauty of human dignity.

Wong, Janet S. and Stacey Schuett, illustrator. *Alex and the Wednesday Chess Club*

Chess, usually seen as a game for eggheads, is shown for what it really is in Wong's universe: a highly competitive sport. Alex, who was humiliated once before, must overcome his self-defeating image of himself in order to develop his fortitude and mental prowess.

BOOKS FOR THE UPPER ELEMENTARY GRADES (GRADES 3–5)

Coville, Bruce. *My Teacher Is an Alien* series

These books are stupid. And that's a compliment. This insane, tongue-in-cheek, intentionally silly series of sci-fi tales has delighted boys and girls alike. Many teachers dislike the series, but if these wacky tales get kids reading, then I'm all for them.

Gantos, Jack. *Joey Pigza* series

Gantos has created a unique antihero, Joey, who is lovable even as his life story is hard to bear. Joey has ADD and his out-of-control behavior hurts him and others. His dysfunctional family only makes things worse. Medication helps him regain control but it doesn't make his family any better. This is a powerful series about a child who is trying to fight both inner demons and outer ones. High-spirited boys will identify with Joey's struggles; others hopefully will gain more sympathy.

Gurney, James, author and illustrator. *Dinotopia* series

From the journal of Arthur Dennison, Victorian scientist, we learn of the events following the shipwreck that left the explorer and his son Will on an uncharted island where dinosaurs and humans live in harmony. The series is accompanied by "Dennison's" sketches—beautiful images that will inspire children and adults alike.

Hale, Bruce. *Chet Gecko Mystery* series

The kind of silliness offered in this series is precious. The wordplay alone will boost your child's literacy skills, and the comic adventures of Chet and his partner Natalie Attired (she's a mockingbird) are sure to enchant many a once-bored reader. Here's another possible benefit: All of the titles are parodies of classic mysteries. As your child gets older he may be tempted to read the originals.

Pilkey, Dav. *Captain Underpants* series

Move over, Superman. This "hero" is really the principal. Transformed by two boys with a toy hypnotism kit, the principal tosses his toupee and runs around in his Titanic tightie-whities doing his best to give superheroes a bad name. This series is the ultimate in gleeful pandemonium.

Sachar, Louis. *Wayside School* series

When Wayside School was built, the architect made a *tiny* mistake. The school does have thirty stories, as requested, but the rooms are stacked one right on top of the other. Life inside the school is as crazy as its design. With one eccentric character after another, Wayside School is home to an engaging series of wacky adventures.

Scieszka, Jon. *Time Warp Trio* series

This comic adventure series includes the original books and published episodes from the TV series. They're jam-packed with witty repartee and hilarious action adventures. Scieszka, a literacy advocate for boys, knows how to charm young male readers.

BOOKS FOR THE MIDDLE GRADES (GRADES 6–8)

Applegate, K.A. *Animorphs* series

A group of children encounters an alien who gives them special powers in order to fight off an impending alien invasion. Each youngster gains the power to transform into a different animal. There's one drawback. If you remain "morphed" for too long (as one unfortunate boy discovers), you're stuck forever with the body of an animal and the mind of a human.

Colfer, Eoin. *Artemis Fowl* series

The ultimate bad boy, archcriminal Artemis Fowl, does battle with Captain Holly Short of the LEPrecon (Lower Elements Police Reconnaissance) Squad. This criminal caper series throws in the kitchen sink, with everything from fairies to electric gadgets. (Fairies with motorized wings?!)

Curtis, Christopher Paul
Curtis's historical fiction tells of the struggles of African Americans. If you want to broaden your children's minds and expand their hearts, these are the stories to do it.

Bud, Not Buddy
Bud Caldwell's mother is dead. He has no living relatives left in the world. Or does he? His mother had a cherished flier depicting a popular jazz musician. Could this be Bud's father? The ten-year-old sets out on a journey to find his roots and we follow him into the treacherous world of the Great Depression.

The Watsons Go to Birmingham, 1963
Byron Watson gets into so much trouble that his parents decide he should be brought down South for the summer to live with his grandmother. The whole family must prepare for the risky business of "driving while Black" in the deep South. Little do they know they're headed straight toward one of the most horrific events in history—the bombing of an Alabama church and the murder of four little girls. This is the tale of family unity and survival in a nation whose history often belies its ideals.

Dixon, Franklin W. *Hardy Boys* series
Dixon, in case you didn't know, wasn't a real person. This was the pseudonym given to the numerous authors-for-hire who cranked out the books under a name that was as fictional as the two protagonists. Frank and Joe, two intrepid brothers, solve puzzle after puzzle in this ever-popular mystery series.

Drake, Emily. *The Magickers* series
Eleven-year-old Jason arrives at Ravenwing, where young people learn magic and fight the forces of evil. Jason soon finds himself in the middle of the battle and must save Ravenwing from destruction. This is a great series for kids who aren't yet up to the literary complexities of Harry Potter. Drake is no J. K. Rowling, but the series certainly has entertainment value.

Eddings, David. The *Tamuli* series

This fantasy series features a classic hero, the knight Sparhawk, who defends his kingdom against evil magic.

Funke, Cornelia. *The Thief Lord*

Orphans Prosper and Bo have run away, refusing to be split up as their sour aunt wishes. As a detective searches for them, the brothers find sanctuary in an abandoned movie theater in Venice, where a ragtag band of runaways has taken refuge. Led by the mysterious Thief Lord, the children become embroiled in a secret plot to find a mystical merry-go-round with revitalizing powers (an eccentric twist on the fountain of youth). This is a strange, touching, and exotic tale from a German author whose sales are second only to J. K. Rowling in Germany.

Hearn, Lian. *Tales of the Otori* series

For kids who are ready to move up from anime, this is a perfect series. Like many graphic novels and anime series, Hearn's tales seem to be set in medieval Japan and yet it's also a fantasy series. Martial-arts battles and supernatural skirmishes add to the appeal of this colorful series.

Horowitz, Anthony. *Alex Rider* series

Horowitz's popular teen spy is the James Bond of the adolescent set. This series brilliantly recreates the tone of Ian Fleming's classic Cold War series (and others in the genre) while still making itself relevant to contemporary teens. This series serves up one thrill after another.

The Gatekeepers series. Troubled teen Matt Freeman is placed in foster care with a sinister and possibly murderous guardian. He uncovers a plot to open a gate that will release a hellish demon. The entire series follows Matt and several other youngsters as they try to prevent additional gates, hidden around the world, from opening.

Korman, Gordon. *Island* series

It's *Survivor* for the middle-school set. Six shipwrecked teens, each with a quirky personality, must pull together to survive one threat after another.

Lewis, C. S. *Chronicles of Narnia*

Hide-and-go-seek never had such amazing results. Four English children, sent to a country house to escape the German blitzkrieg, discover that at the back of an armoire there's an entrance to a magical world. Like the adults in the outer world, they are drawn into a battle between good and evil where they must use all their wits and courage. Originally planned as a series of Christian parables, these tales can be used to teach children about ethical choices with or without the religious subtext.

Paulsen, Gary. *Hatchet* series

The series begins with a plane crash. Brian Robeson, whose pilot has died, is left to fend for himself in the wilderness with only a hatchet. This teen Robinson Crusoe survives on wits and guts while developing a symbiotic relationship with the untamed world around him.

Rodda, Emily. *Deltora Quest* series

This is a classic good-versus-evil fantasy series. The exotic settings and characters will give young readers many a literary thrill.

Rook, Sebastian. *Vampire Plagues* series

It's the Artful Dodger meets Dracula! Jack Harkett, a London street urchin, is prowling the docks when he meets Ben, a disheveled young swell who, having escaped a mysterious frigate, tells a tale of horror. Together, the boys will travel across continents battling a plague of vampires that feed on the blood of the living. Rook is a master at creating atmosphere of the spookiest kind.

Rowling, J. K. Harry Potter series

You'd have to be an ignorant Muggle not to know this series. Rowling's high-end fantasy novels about a loser who becomes a hero wizard is the most popular children's series in history. Life at Hogwarts, the school for wizards, grows increasingly menacing with each episode, as *He Who Must Not Be Named* tries to conquer the world. Harry must defeat him at every turn or be destroyed.

Shan, Darren. *Cirque Du Freak* series

Darren Shan is the name of the author and the main character of the series. Darren narrates his adventures in a weird circus sideshow where vampires and other supernatural menaces abound. Darren's dark adventures are bloody good fun.

Snicket, Lemony. *A Series of Unfortunate Events*

For those of you who have seen the silent films *Orphans of the Storm* and *The Perils of Pauline*, this series will be quite familiar. The books are send-ups of the damsel-in-distress genre, only here it's three wealthy orphans in distress. And they're being pursued by the evil Count Olaf who's after their money.

Stine, R. L. *Goosebumps* series

Before J. K. Rowling there was R. L. Stine, whose spooky tales were gobbled up by kids all over the country. *Goosebumps* books continue to line the shelves of chain stores everywhere. Their shivery plots never fail to delight.

Strasser, Tod

Help! I'm Trapped **series.** Strasser, author of the films *Home Alone* and *Ferris Bueller's Day Off*, has written a fantasy series in which a youngster gets trapped inside the bodies of various adults. This series takes the concept of walking in someone else's shoes to bizarre and hilarious heights. A note of warning: Some adults love the repartee in this series; others find the put-down humor offensive.

DriftX **series.** This is darker then the *Help! I'm Trapped* series. Japanese-American Kennin discovers a talent for drag-racing. The seventeen-year-old daredevil finds himself involved in danger and crime as he gets more and more involved in the world of high-risk competition. Being cool has its risks.

Van Draanen, Wendelin. *Shredderman* series

Nerdy Nolan is tired of being bullied; thus, his alter ego is born: Shredderman, a cyber muckraker with a gift for exposing the truth.

BOOKS FOR HIGH SCHOOL (GRADES 9–12)

Applegate, K.A. *Everworld* series

When we dream, it sometimes seems like we've entered another world. What if it really happened?

Draper, Sharon M. *Tears of a Tiger*

If you're worried about the dangers of teens who drink and drive, this is a powerful book to read with your child. Andy, the protagonist, cannot get over the guilt of his friend's death. He was driving drunk the night they crashed. Robert was killed. This is a tough tale of two lives destroyed by drunk driving.

Flinn, Alex. *Breathing Underwater*

When his psychological abuse of his girlfriend escalates into physical violence, Nick Andreas is forced by a judge to attend anger-management classes. Slowly, Nick is compelled to confront the past that turned him into a monster. But is his growing self-awareness enough to save him from his own destructive impulses?

Gardner, Graham. *Inventing Elliot*

Teased all his life for his nerdiness, Elliot Sutton reinvents himself when he arrives at Holminster High. His cool reserve makes him popular for the first time in his life, but the teens who embrace him belong to an elite, secret society of vicious bullies.

Elliot has succeeded in reinventing himself, but at what price? Will he transform into a heartless aggressor, or will he find his integrity, even if it means that once again he'll be a victim?

Herbert, Frank. *Dune* series

When his universe is shattered by political turmoil, young Paul Atreides becomes a refugee on a desert planet. Thus begins this classic sci-fi series, which is as futuristic as any yet at the same time has the grand sweep of a medieval saga or even the Bible itself. For Paul may be more than a mere boy. He may be a savior, a messiah of the future world.

Hobbs, Will

Hobbs is a master of the outdoor action-adventure genre. His young antiheroes may not always be models of propriety, but they're invariably models of bravery and resourcefulness.

Downriver. At a camp called Discovery Unlimited, a group of young thugs are expected to develop stronger values by braving the wilderness. But for these youngsters, the controlled thrills of Discovery are not enough. Stealing a raft, they brave the rapids of the Colorado River, embarking on a hair-raising journey of danger and self-discovery.

Jason's Gold. Jason's brothers have left Seattle to search for gold in Alaska. Jason, unwilling to be left behind, faces one obstacle after another as he crosses the wilderness in search of his family. This work of historical fiction features real people and events from the Gold Rush days.

The Maze. Rick, a reform-school runaway, finds himself lost in the canyons of Utah where he meets Lon Peregrino, a naturalist and loner who is trying to save the dwindling condor population. Lon teaches Rick how to hang glide, a skill that comes in handy when he must battle local radicals with a deadly secret.

Myers, Walter Dean. *Slam!*
Greg Harris, better known as Slam on the basketball courts, is a poor student who feels like a fish out of water in his new school. As he tries to negotiate his social world, his grandmother's illness, and his floundering grades, Slam also tries to struggle his way upward in the very uncertain game of life.

Paolini, Christopher. *Eldest* series
Paolini, who published the first volume at the tender age of eighteen, has given us an intricate adventure series featuring Eragon, a young dragon rider, and Saphira, the dragon he raised from infancy. Think Luke Skywalker on a dragon. This is the sort of epic adventure that avid fantasy readers love to get lost in.

Sanchez, Alex. *Rainbow* series
Realistic, honest, painful, and uplifting, this series follows the lives of a group of gay teens through all sorts of struggles, from romances to coming out to embracing political activism. If you have a gay teen, these books are great for starting a dialogue. If your child is straight, these books are great tools for teaching compassion.

Stine, R. L. *Fear Street* series
The popular *Goosebumps* author offers this series for older teens. These tales of suspense seem right out of the radio thrillers of the 1940s, with a generous dollop of teen angst added in.

Stroud, Jonathan. *The Bartimaeus Trilogy*
Nathaniel, an apprentice wizard, summons the jinni Bartimaeus to help him defeat a bully. The results: unexpected mayhem. Throughout the thrilling series, Nathaniel encounters dark supernatural forces and must protect London from evil magic.

Tolkien, J.R.R. *The Lord of the Rings*

This is one of the most popular of fantasy series ever written, recently given new life in the movies. Hobbit Frodo is charged with a grave duty: carry a ring created by the Dark Lord (no, not Valdemort, another fellow called Sauron) and cast it into the Crack of Doom. This, the ultimate quest tale, is filled with fantasy languages and fully imagined fantastical terrain.

Wells, H.G.

Wells remains one of the great sci-fi novelists of all times. His tales are fast-paced, gripping, and filled with delectable horror. You might find it fun to discuss some of the themes that run through his novels. Among these are:

- Mad scientists
- The domination of one race by another
- Evil in paradise
- Cannibalism
- The benefits and drawbacks of science (a classic theme in science fiction)

The First Men in the Moon. In Victorian England, Professor Cavor and his worldlier companion, Bedford, use the professor's antigravity technique to reach the moon. There, they discover the Selenites, an intelligent but dangerous race of insects. It's a race for survival as the two earthmen scramble to escape the alien insects while enduring the harsh lunar environment.

The Invisible Man. There's a new lodger at the Coach and Horses. He's swaddled in bandages, never showing his face or hands. Griffin is in fact the ultimate mad scientist. Having turned himself invisible, he cannot reverse the process. When he ultimately loses his mind, he goes on a murderous rampage. Who can defeat a killer who cannot be seen?

The Island of Dr. Moreau. This is a Darwinian tale of horror in which a shipwrecked man discovers an island paradise in which animals have been transformed, by a mad scientist, into perversions of humanity.

The Time Machine. In this tale, Wells begins yet another genre—the time travel story. The protagonist, known only as the Time Traveler, journeys to the year 8---, where he discovers the Eloi, a placid race of vegetarians. Their lives are hardly idyllic. They are periodically devoured by the Morlocks, a race of subterranean cannibals. The Time Traveler tries to help the Eloi and recapture his machine, which the Morlocks have stolen.

War of the Worlds. Every alien invasion story owes its existence to this, the first of its genre. Still gripping, this is the tale of cannibalistic Martians who invade Earth and blast their way across the planet with their spider-like war machines—still one of the most haunting images in the literature of the fantastic.

Westerfeld, Scott. *Midnighters* series
When she moves to the town of Bixby, Oklahoma, Jessica Day discovers a secret, one that very few people know. Tucked in between midnight and 12:01 A.M. is an extra hour—a supernatural span of time populated by strange creatures called Darklings. These supernatural beasts have remained harmless until Jessica arrives. Now, they want her dead. Jessica and a band of gifted teens must discover the secret behind the Darklings' attacks or Bixby will become the hub of a supernatural invasion.

Wooding, Chris. *Kerosene*
Cal, painfully shy and socially awkward, gets picked on a lot. He relieves his frustrations through his favorite activity—pyromania. But when, for sport, one of the school's most popular girls decides to toy with his affections, Cal's barely suppressed rage turns into an emotional inferno—with potentially deadly results.

Graphic Novels

We live in a visual age. Our kids' senses are saturated with TV, video games, computer games, and the like. Even teen clothing is saturated with imagery. Our visual culture has impacted the literary world—big time! Many chain bookstores now have sections devoted entirely to graphic novels.

Too many adults try to steer their children away from these. This is a mistake. Even if a graphic novel is light on the number of words, it's still a book with characters and conflicts. Kids read them, think about them, discuss them, even trade them. And many teens who like graphic novels build their concentration and then willingly accept the challenge of reading more traditional books.

Spend time with your child browsing through the graphic novel section of your local bookstore or library. There is a constant flow of new graphic novels on the shelves, so shopping for these books can become an ongoing family adventure. Instead of chastising your child for his interest in these books, encourage him; then try to find traditional novels on related topics. It's likely that he'll shuttle back and forth between graphic and standard novels. This is fine.

Please be aware that the content of many graphic novels is strong. This is another reason why you want to review them with your child. You can use the selection process as a way of teaching your family's value system. You can veto those of which you don't approve, or you can use the strong content as a launching point for family discussions (as you can do with any book).

There are two additional issues with graphic novels. First, they're expensive. Producing all of that imagery tends to pump up the prices. So if money's an issue, find what you like in the bookstore, and then ask your librarian to order the books. Also, many graphic novels are parts of long series. If your child likes a book, he will probably become fanatical about reading the entire series. Again, either your bookstore or library might have to order the series.

Aki, Katsu. *Psychic Academy*

Ai Shiomi, the hero of this series, is pressured into attending a training school for psychic children. He lives in the shadow of his brother, a celebrated psychic and teacher at the school.

Akino, Matsuri. *Pet Shop of Horrors*

As the saying goes, "Be careful what you wish for; you may get it." Count D is a transvestite and owner of a weird pet shop where people go to buy mystical animals—creatures that can make your dreams come true. But when your wishes come true there's often an unexpected and unsettling price to pay.

Aragonés, Sergio. *Groo Inferno*

"The road to hell," they say, "is paved with good intentions." In this collection of four novels from the series, would-be hero Groo is a comic bumbler whose efforts to help others lead to hilarious disasters.

Arakawa, Hiromu. *Fullmetal Alchemist*

Two brothers, Edward and Alphonse, have dabbled in alchemy with disastrous results. Edward has lost two limbs and Alphonse has lost his entire body, becoming a soul encased in armor. Now they've been drawn into the government's military complex where good and evil forces compete to find and possess the legendary Philosopher's Stone.

Busiek, Kurt. *Astro City: Life in the Big City*

This series is the *Grand Hotel* of graphic novels, with a variety of odd characters coming in and out of the narrative. The real hero is the city itself, a mythical town where superheroes and "normal" folks intermingle. There's even a neighborhood called Shadow Hill, a shuddery place where the supernatural world takes up its residence.

Collins, Max Allen, Sam Mendes, and Richard Piers Rayner. *The Road to Perdition*

Move over Tony Soprano. This dark tale of gangland violence centers around Michael O'Sullivan, a mob assassin. When Michael's son sees him take part in a hit, Michael's associates decide to eliminate him and his entire family. Michael's wife and younger son are killed and the plot escalates into a bloody tale of revenge.

Gaiman, Neil and various illustrators. *The Sandman* **series**
This series has everything from a teenage girl who dresses Goth-style (she's really Death) to a creature with teeth in his eye sockets to a convention for serial killers. Gaiman's tales, which take place in a mythical dream world, are beyond dark.

Higuchi, Daisuke. *Whistle!*
Sho is short and a second-string soccer player, but what he lacks in stature he makes up for in determination. He's a little tiger who proves that with the right attitude anyone can "bend it like Beckham."

Lim, Kara and Lee Chi Hyong. *Demon Diary*
For ages, the gods and demons have battled, but a prophecy says that one will be born who will unite the enemies. This is Raenef, who will become a great leader if he can learn wisdom from Eclipse, his tutor. Unfortunately Raenef is somewhat lacking in common sense.

Judal. *Vampire Game*
Duzell is a tomcat cub. He's also the reincarnation of the Vampire King. Talk about a kitten with a whip! Duzell seeks revenge on Phelios, who killed him in a previous lifetime. Now, as he searches for the reincarnation of his old enemy, Duzell has become a pet to Ishtar, Phelios' great-granddaughter. This series is a whirlwind of intrigue with a good deal of humor thrown in.

Miller, Frank. *The Dark Knight Returns*
This resurrected and re-envisioned telling of the *Batman* tale is notable for its brilliant artwork and dark portrait of an urban environment gone mad.

Moore, Alan and David Lloyd. *V for Vendetta*
This is a nightmarish portrait of what the world might become. England has been overrun by a totalitarian regime. The mysterious V, avenger or terrorist depending on the reader's point of view, wreaks havoc on the Fascists who now run the country.

Moore, Alan and Dave Gibbons. *Watchmen*

An acclaimed and sophisticated series, *Watchmen* is the tale of the Crimebusters, a team of superheroes. Somebody is trying to wipe them out of existence. As good battles evil in classic comic-book style, the creators offer a surprising degree of sophistication by linking commentaries and historical notes to the main text. This is a great series for teaching young readers how to use text features.

Moore, Alan and Kevin O'Neill. *The League of Extraordinary Gentlemen*

Several characters from nineteenth-century gothic literature, including the Invisible Man and Jekyll and Hyde, have been gathered together, and before you can say "public domain" they are woven into a band of superheroes. This series might tempt your child into reading the original novels from which the characters are taken.

Ohkami, Mineko. *Dragon Knights*

This series blends action-adventure with eccentric characters and humorous quips. The three knights of the title compete with each other as well as with their enemies.

Sakai, Stan. *Usagi Yojimbo: Grasscutter*

Usagi Yojimbo is no White Rabbit. Yes, he's a bunny, but he's also a ronin, an independent samurai living in feudal Japan, battling evil enemies of the animal kingdom. Usagi wanders from place to place hiring out his services and battling his way from adventure to adventure. Many of the episodes in the series read as stand-alone short stories, but the series can also be viewed as a saga.

Seto, Andy. *Crouching Tiger, Hidden Dragon* (adapted from the novels of Wang du Lu)

Following the success of the film version of du Lu's first novel, Seto has produced a series of graphic novels. As the series begins, Yu Shu Lien is threatened by the dangerous warrior Golden

Sword. She meets Lu Mu Bai, a Buddhalike figure who sits on a rock in the middle of a river controlling the currents with his mind. The two are attracted but in great star-crossed-lover tradition, Yu Shu Lien is betrothed to another. Love never goes smoothly in this grand, romantic saga as the tortured romance is tested again and again by fate and by enemies galore.

Shigeno, Shuichi. *Initial D*

It's daredevil stunts galore as Takumi, drag racer extraordinaire, accelerates into a breathtaking and dangerous string of adventures. Readers, start your engines! Parents, *hide your car keys!*

Spiegelman, Art. *Maus: A Survivor's Tale*

This is the most bizarre, compelling, and important graphic novel on the list. Based on his Polish father's harrowing autobiographical account of escaping the Nazis, Spiegelman retells father Vladek's stories, while substituting anthropomorphic images for human ones. (Jewish "mice," for example, are threatened by Nazi "cats.") Rather than trivializing the horrors of the Holocaust, Spiegelman has made the story accessible to young readers while driving home the sheer cruelty of one of history's greatest disgraces.

Takahashi, Rumiko. *InuYasha*

This series takes place in a mythical feudal Japan where demons and heroes battle for supremacy. InuYasha, the dog-boy hero of the series, is part human, part demon but his sympathies lie with the human race.

Toriyama, Akira. *Dragon Ball Z*

This is *the* series, at least in my home. Throughout his early teens, my son Kenny claimed the title of "greatest *Dragon Ball Z* fan in the world." He often daydreamed (as thousands of boys probably have) of being Goku, the hero of the series. The books have given rise to a popular TV series and a string of video games. In this saga, there are seven magical balls—Dragon Balls—spread out across the world. If they are gathered together, the person possessing them can summon Shenron, the Eternal Dragon, who will grant one wish. The problem is that Goku's not the only one searching for the Dragon Balls. There's a host of evil characters trying to gather them together.

Yuy, Beop-Ryong and Hui-jin-Park. *Chronicles of the Cursed Sword*

Moosunge, who has been corrupted by a deceitful prime minister, attempts with the aid of his living PaChun Sword to assassinate his own brother, the Emperor. Enter Rey Yan with a magical sword of his own, PaSa Sword. With the aid of his sister Shyao, Rey Yan battles would-be conquerors and demons. It's good sword versus evil sword in this mystical saga.

CHAPTER 12

Learning Disabilities: What to Know and What to Do

There are many types of learning disabilities, many of which can be helped. Often, moderate to significant improvement is possible. It is important to understand that learning disabled doesn't mean stupid. Many disabilities are not intellectual. They're physiological. Some have clear causes and many are still under investigation.

Please understand that if you have a child with a disability it's neither a disgrace nor a blot on your reputation as a parent. Many learning disabilities are no worse than being born with impaired hearing or fallen arches. Your ultimate goal is to make certain that your child gets the best possible support from you, from her teachers, and from any service providers you may engage.

The Challenge of Learning Disabilities

One of the biggest challenges of learning disabilities is the fact that they're often hard to detect. People can struggle for a long time (sometimes a lifetime) without having their disabilities diagnosed. The longer this continues, the more these individuals feel like failures. Then the problem gets worse because depression, if it wasn't present already, becomes part of the mix.

Many people have a mistaken belief that failure in school is due to laziness or a bad attitude. Often what appears to be laziness is really an undetected disability. It's not that a child won't do her work, it's that she *can't*. Resistance is often an expression of frustration and even of self-loathing. Children with undetected disabilities bear a heavy emotional burden.

In order to help children succeed in school, we need to move away from a culture of blame. We must make sure that if there are any disabilities, they are diagnosed. We must be certain that the appropriate services are provided. Then we must make our children accountable in ways that are developmentally appropriate.

For example, if a child has a low reading level, we don't pressure her to read books that are way above her present capability. We do make her accountable for practicing her reading skills in an appropriate text on her level. The trick is to get organized and provide whatever supports we can at home; when more is needed, we need to seek help.

And for heaven's sake don't be embarrassed to ask for help. A learning disability is not a discredit to your parenting. It's a chance occurrence. Students aren't disabled, in most cases, because of bad parenting. Sometimes, yes, but mostly, no. Besides, if you're reading this book you're probably a very caring parent, so if you suspect your child has a learning disability lighten up on yourself. Get help for your child and start to formulate a plan of action. Action is the first step toward giving a disabled child a better future.

When learning disabilities come into play, special education services may become necessary. Along with helping your child at home, part of your job as a parent will be to become your child's educational advocate. Some districts will be very helpful in your quest for services, others will not. Special education costs a lot and many districts will avoid providing these costly services. Others will overprescribe services, placing children into highly restrictive special education classes when moderate intervention plans would do the trick.

The Overuse of Special Education

When you look at the numbers, you will find there is a major overrepresentation of two groups in special education. Your child is more likely to be diagnosed as needing special education if he falls into one of two categories: male or black. According to a study published by Western Michigan University:

> Subjective and unreliable identification procedures have . . . been associated with the overrepresentation of African American males in special education. Teacher referrals along with testing are the primary measures used to identify whether or not a student is in need of special education services. Each of these measures poses unique challenges to the crisis of the frequent placement of African American males in special education. Both methods have questionable reliability and have been critiqued for their use.

Here's the difficult trick. Black or white, male or female, if your child is having trouble in school it may be a serious emotional problem or it may not. On the other hand, some district leaders will rail against placing children in special education when their real goal is to save money. There's an old saying, *The devil mixes lies with truth.* Sometimes, the devil works in your district office. So what's a parent to do?

First of all, if you think your child has a problem, demand that he be tested. Put your demand in writing and send it to your child's principal from the post office with a return receipt requested. Make sure the letter has a date on it, by the way. It wouldn't hurt to have the letter notarized, either. Keep the receipt and a copy of the letter in a file folder. Keep the folder in a safe place. Hang on to this folder and all of its future contents for the rest of your child's school career. This means up to and including graduate school.

Yes, that's right: through graduate school. If it turns out your child indeed has a learning disability, he will be entitled to legal services at every educational level. *Never lose any documentation.* You never know when it will be needed.

If your child is to read well and think well, you must become a good advocate, demanding appropriate services from your school and district while providing additional support at home. This chapter will describe some of the most common learning disabilities, the treatments schools can provide, and, most importantly, the things you can do at home to help your child move toward success.

Expressive Language Disorders

Expressive language disorders have many symptoms. Children might have difficulty pronouncing words or communicating clearly. They may hear people speaking to them but they might not make sense out of what is being said. The term *expressive language disorder* describes a problem that can range from a lisp to an inability to express oneself in more than a few brief words or phrases.

Experts divide expressive language disorders into two categories: speech disorders and language disorders.

Here are some questions to help you identify possible speech disorders:

- Does my child substitute one sound for another? (I offer a word of caution here. Most young children mispronounce words. If there are many more mispronunciations than other children of the same age, that's when you should be concerned. So don't jump the gun.)
- Does my child have trouble pronouncing things clearly—is there a lisp or some other impediment?
- Does my child stutter or stumble when speaking?
- Does my child have difficulty speaking or reading aloud in a smooth, expressive manner? Does he speak in a monotone or have difficulty expressing ideas using the natural rise and fall of speech?

Here are some questions to help you identify a possible language disorder:

- Does my child have difficulty recalling the names of objects?
- Does he babble when trying to express something because he can't pull the right words out of his brain?
- Does my child frequently use the wrong names for the things he's talking about?
- Does my child have difficulty following the basic grammatical rules that other children his age can follow?
- Does my child have difficulty remembering the meanings of words, even those he's heard many times?

Following is a sample letter that a parent might write to the school principal. Notice that the letter is very specific when identifying the problem. It is also clear and to-the-point in what it asks for. Avoid offering a possible diagnosis. Leave that to the professionals. Also, although most requests for special services happen in elementary school, your child is entitled to special services at any age.

Dr. Julia Harkness, Principal
The Phyllis Wheatley School
301 Potter Avenue
Staten Island, New York 11368

Dear Dr. Harkness:

My daughter Crystal is in Mrs. Bailey's first-grade class at Phyllis Wheatley. She's not doing well in reading though she tries very hard. I've noticed that Crystal has difficulty remembering the meanings of new words, even after she's been told the meaning many times. Often she uses the wrong words to describe things. In the supermarket, last week, she pointed to a grapefruit and said, "Buy apple." She's learned the word *grapefruit* but never seems to remember.

I would like Crystal to be tested to see if she has any learning disabilities. I look forward to meeting with you within thirty business days. Please let me know if a 9 A.M. meeting on December 12 is convenient. You can send that information along with the written report to the address above. To set up the appointment, please send me a confirmation letter or call me at the number above.

Thanks for your attention in this matter.

Sincerely yours,
Tiffany Langford

It's always best to catch expressive language disorders as early as possible. If remediation starts early, there will be fewer problems at school. If your child has not yet reached school age, then your pediatrician is the first person to approach. You don't have to mail a letter if you're approaching a doctor, but I would still encourage you to write down your concerns and bring them, and your child, to the doctor's office. She will likely refer you to a specialist for further testing.

Following is a description of *developmental milestones*—the developments you can expect at various stages of early childhood. This is a rough guideline. Children don't develop at exactly the same rate, but if there are significant gaps that haven't closed for quite some time, then it couldn't hurt to consult with your pediatrician.

What you can expect at approximately six months of age:
- Your child will be producing lots of vowel sounds and some consonants. These sounds will often be expressions of delight produced during play.
- Your child will produce cooing sounds when familiar adults are seen or heard nearby.
- Your child will make sounds to catch your attention.

What you can expect at twelve months of age:
- Your child's sounds will not yet be articulate but they will begin to sound a little more like real speech.
- Your child will begin to understand a modest vocabulary of about one hundred words.
- Using this new vocabulary, your child will be able to respond to simple play commands such as "Where is your nose?" or "Touch your toes."
- If asked, your child will be able to point to objects, when asked questions such as "Where's the doggie?"
- Your child will begin to ask for things or people using single words such as "Dada."

What you can expect at approximately eighteen months of age:
- Your child should be using a greater number of single words—roughly a dozen of them.
- When making sounds and attempting to use simple words, your child will begin to point at objects to express his needs.

What you can expect at approximately two years of age:
- Your child will begin combining words: "Want juice," or "My Teddy."
- Your child knows and can say his own name.
- Your child can sit and listen to stories in picture books. He can point to and identify characters in favorite books.
- Your child has developed a spoken vocabulary of roughly three hundred words.

What you can expect at approximately three years of age:
- Your child can speak simple sentences of three to four words or more.
- Your child can describe situations and express feelings and ideas—a complicated and miraculous skill.
- Your child can understand and express time concepts such as lunchtime, dinnertime, or yesterday and tomorrow.
- Your child can point to and name colors.
- Your child can remember and recite his address.
- Your child can tell a story or retell an experience. He won't always get the events in perfect order.
- Your child can sing songs and recite nursery rhymes.
- Your child can begin counting numbers.

If you have concerns, bring the above chart to your pediatrician and explain to her the events you're not seeing. Once the testing has been done, you'll get a clearer picture of your child's needs.

Receptive Language Disorders

Receptive language disorders are often symptoms of other disorders. This is why you need professional help to sort out exactly what's going on. Here are some potential areas of concern that you might want to bring to the attention of your child's school or pediatrician. Ask yourself the following:

- Does my child constantly repeat or parrot words or phrases when another person is talking to him?
- Does my child give odd or off-base responses to questions?

- Does my child have a hard time answering simple questions requiring a "yes" or "no" answer?
- Does my child have difficulty answering critical thinking questions, such as the classic 5 Ws (Who? What? When? Where? Why?)?
- Does my child speak in garbled or unintelligible words and phrases?

There are a variety of possible causes of receptive language disorders. Some can be diagnosed; others are mysterious. Science still has large gaps where learning disabilities are concerned. To add to the confusion, there are a lot of myths floating around. The latest one I've heard is that some learning disabilities are caused by vaccines. I don't know of any conclusive studies that prove this to be true. It's best to speak to your pediatrician and school psychologist for good information. It can never hurt to get a second opinion, either, but don't go to your know-it-all neighbor down the street. Speak to a qualified professional.

Here's what we do know about receptive language disorders:

- They're sometimes caused by simple hearing and vision
- problems. If your child has a hearing impairment, even a mild one, he may have trouble distinguishing between sounds. This can impact his comprehension in conversations and in reading.
- Visual impairments prevent children from picking up the physical and facial clues that add to their understanding of spoken language.
- If your child has any problems maintaining attention, then a lot of information will escape him. This will have a huge impact on his ability to understand both spoken and written English.
- If your child has any sort of memory problems, he will have difficulties in two areas. First, he'll struggle to connect the combinations of sounds needed to understand spoken and written English. Second, he won't be able to hold facts in his head and therefore he'll get lost when listening to people or

reading stories. This is a classic case of why phonics alone can't always help young readers. Unless the memory problem is fixed, neither phonics nor comprehension lessons will be retained.

If you suspect your child has a receptive language disorder, here are some of the tests you can expect. Don't assume (especially if you're asking your child's school for help) that these things will automatically be done. Ask for them. Remember, some districts want to save money at your child's expense. They're counting on your lack of knowledge. If you explicitly ask for tests, you're more likely to get them.

When a child is suspected of having a receptive language disorder, these are some of the tests you can expect:

A hearing test, conducted by a professional audiologist, will help determine whether or not there's a hearing impairment. A professional hearing test should include an *audio processing assessment.* This enables the audiologist to determine if your child can pay attention to sounds or distinguish among sounds. Often, a child who appears to have "normal" hearing actually has one of these problems. Sadly, these problems are often mistaken for laziness or stupidity. An audio processing assessment can clear up such misconceptions.

A vision test is vital. I can attest to this from personal experience. During the first months of second grade, I was often berated by my mother for failing to copy all my homework. She checked my notebook regularly (a good thing) and noticed that my homework and class notes were poorly copied. Fortunately, after a few months my mother began to suspect what was really going on. She brought me to an eye doctor and it turned out that I was (and still am) nearsighted. I needed glasses. A simple eye exam transformed my school performance. A trip to the ophthalmologist might help your child, too.

A speech pathologist can test your child for any impairment. What the pathologist can do is compare your child's test results against the typical skill level of children at various ages. This will help the pathologist determine if there are any problems present.

A psychologist can conduct a series of tests to see if there are any comprehension problems. A psychologist or a school's educational evaluator can also observe your child in class to see how he functions in his learning environment. Usually when this is done, the observer avoids telling a child that he is the one being observed. This way, your child won't change his typical behavior.

Psychological tests also help to determine whether or not a social or emotional problem is present. It is possible that you will be asked to provide a family history as well. This can be uncomfortable. We can all feel vulnerable when discussing the ups and downs of our families' lives. Try to bear with it. A social history isn't supposed to be a *gotcha*. It's an opportunity to provide the specialists with information that can help your child.

Dyslexia

First off, let's clear away what dyslexia is not. It's not low IQ. It's not laziness. Sadly, parents and teachers all too often mistake this puzzling disability for a moral or intellectual failing. Kids with dyslexia are generally just as bright as—sometimes brighter than—others. They can't show it because their disability masks their underlying brain power.

There are many dyslexic kids (and adults) throughout the country. Many fall by the wayside. If you suspect that your child is one of these children, speak to your school or pediatrician. Here are some questions you may want to consider:

- Is my child a year old and still not talking?
- Is my child three years or older and struggling to speak?
- Does my child substitute some sounds for others, such as *killow* instead of *pillow* or *buppy* instead of *puppy*?
- Does my child stutter?
- Does my child have trouble distinguishing right from left?

- Does my child have lots of trouble learning to tie his shoelaces?
- Does my child (after the age of four or five) have difficulty identifying words that rhyme even if he's heard the same nursery rhymes over and over?
- Does my child have difficulty pronouncing the letters *r, l, m,* and *n?*
- Does my child use different hands for different activities, such as the right hand for writing but the left hand for throwing a ball?

If your child is already in school and learning to read, you can ask his teacher the following:

- Does my child have trouble remembering words that he's read and learned on previous pages?
- Does my child have trouble learning phonics skills? Does he resist any attempts to get him to use phonics in reading unfamiliar words?
- Does my child leave out letters when reading a word?
- When reading a word, does my child add letters that aren't there?
- Does my child have poor fluency? In other words, does he fail to read aloud smoothly and with expression? Does he miss the natural rises and falls of written language? Does he miss the changes in rhythm indicated by punctuation marks?
- When writing, does my child confuse any of the following pairs: b-d, b-p, m-w, n-u?
- Does my child have difficulty remembering the spelling of even the simplest words, even if he's practiced them over and over?
- Does he misspell words copied directly from the chalkboard or a book?
- Does my child's ability to retell a story or an experience seem much stronger than his ability to read a story?

Dysgraphia

Dysgraphia is a subcategory of dyslexia. Don't worry about the terminology. Focus more on the symptoms. If you answer yes to any of the following, alert your school or pediatrician.

- Does my child have difficulty holding a pencil or crayon? Does he hold writing implements in his fist rather than the normal way?
- Does my child get muscle cramps because he holds his writing implements so tightly? Does he have to rub, flex, or shake his writing hand because it gets sore?
- Does my child have difficulty writing on the lines of his paper?
- Does my child have difficulty staying within the margins of his paper?
- Does my child write words and letters that are either too far apart or so close that one word can't be distinguished from another?
- Does my child get headaches when reading or writing?
- Does my child complain that the words on the page seem to move? (No, he's not "just seeing things.")

Here's some good news. Children with dyslexia can, with professional help, become stronger readers. Special services won't make them smarter, because in most cases they already have good intellectual skills. Special services, if competently delivered, can help your child grow better at demonstrating his already-present intelligence by writing and reading well.

Here's some more good news. As the saying goes, *God giveth and God taketh away*. Those who are born dyslexic have brains that work differently from the general population. While reading and writing is a struggle, dyslexic children are often *better* than others in certain areas. Dyslexic children are often better at:

- Art
- Music
- Athletics
- Mechanical skills
- Interpersonal communication

Moving Forward after a Diagnosis

So you've been through the tests and your child has been diagnosed with some form of dyslexia. What can you expect? What should you ask for? You should request (if necessary, demand) that your school district provide Orton-Gillingham style training or another multi-sensory approach to literacy instruction.

What are these? The Orton-Gillingham method was developed by Dr. Samuel Orton and psychologist Anna Gillingham in the 1930s. Their goal was to create a scientific and systematic approach to training dyslexics. Since dyslexics have difficulties reading with just their eyes, Orton and Gillingham experimented with new teaching methods that included all of the senses. Many programs today use the methods developed by Orton and Gillingham; or they use other multi-sensory techniques to help children learn to read.

If your child receives such training, here are some of the steps involved:

- Your child will learn to hear the sounds in different words before he ever learns to read them.
- Once your child has developed a measure of competence in hearing sounds (called phonemic awareness), he will begin to learn the connections between sounds and individual letters and sounds and combinations of letters. He might, for example, learn to distinguish between the "t" sound and the "d" sound and then move on to learning the two sounds made by the letter combination *th*.
- Your child will then be explicitly taught the different types of syllables that exist in the English language. For example, he will learn that the *i* in smile is always pronounced as a long vowel because the syllable ends with a consonant followed by a silent *e*.

- Next, your child will learn how to use root words, prefixes, and suffixes to independently determine the meanings of many unfamiliar words.
- Throughout the process, your child will be exposed to multisensory approaches to learning sounds, words, and syllables. These may include such techniques as clapping out syllables or feeling cut-out letters with sandpaper. By feeling the sensation of the letters, your child can recognize their shapes with his fingers. Alone on a page a letter might be hard to remember, but connecting the visual image of the letter to the sensation of its shape may enable your child to recognize that letter in the future when he sees it on a page in a book.
- The instructor will constantly assess whether or not your child is "getting it." If not, he will be retaught as many times as necessary. The instructor will use as many approaches as possible until your child's skills improve.

Once your child has mastered the skills I've just described, he'll be much more prepared to interpret the meaning embedded in texts. There are no guarantees of success, but through multisensory learning the odds will be much greater that your child will learn to read well.

Here's one important thing to remember: The younger your child is when he receives these services, the more likely he is to become a good reader. Older children and even dyslexic adults can benefit from multisensory training, but the training needed will be more intensive, and success, while achievable, will be limited.

ADD/ADHD

Attention deficit disorder (ADD) and attention deficit hyperactivity disorder (ADHD) are neurological disorders. Children with ADD:

- Have a hard time paying attention to tasks, including reading and writing tasks
- Have difficulty completing tasks, including educational tasks

- Are easily bored with all but highly frenetic tasks such as video games or some sporting activities

Children with ADHD may have any or all of the above symptoms. Additionally, they may:

- Lack self-control
- Demonstrate impulsive behavior
- "Bounce off the walls" (show an inability to sit still for any extended period of time)

Be careful with the last point. Many children are mislabeled by teachers. Some are truly ADHD but many merely fall under the category of *boy*. Boys tend to be more kinetic than girls (though not always) and teachers can overreact. If your child is an African American boy, it's even more likely that he'll be mislabeled. According to the *Chronicle of Higher Education* (February 5, 2008):

> Data illustrates that African American students are 2.9 times as likely to be labeled mentally retarded, 1.9 times as likely to labeled seriously emotionally disturbed, and 1.3 times as likely to be labeled as having a learning disability. Black students make up over one-third of all students identified as mentally retarded and one-fourth of those labeled emotionally disturbed. Even more disconcerting are data from states such as Virginia where blacks were reported as 20 percent of the population but constitute over half of the students in programs for the mildly retarded or a state such as Alabama that certifies four times as many minorities as emotionally mentally retarded than whites.

As the child's parent, it's best to assess whether your son's behavior is significantly more chaotic than that of his friends or other boys of his age. This is a good indicator of whether or not you should be concerned.

Also, if you're getting complaints from the teacher, take a day off from work if possible and spend a few hours observing the class. Poor classroom management can be the reason for the "problem." If the teacher is criticizing your child's behavior and most of the class is behaving the same way, the problem is the teacher, not your child. In this case, your task is to put pressure on the principal or, if necessary, the school district, to put your child in another class.

Try to negotiate for a better teacher. If you meet with resistance you may want to see if your community has any local advocacy groups. Very often these are low-cost or even free. It's a sad reality that many children won't get needed services unless their parents fight for them. As they say, *the squeaky wheel gets the oil.*

If you suspect your child might be suffering from ADHD, here are some questions to ask yourself:

- Does my child have difficulty getting along with others, including family members, other children, and teachers?
- Does the trouble often stem from impulsive acts committed by my child because he's failed to think through the consequences of his actions?
- Does my child often forget or lose possessions, including homework and school assignments?
- Does my child have difficulty falling asleep or waking up in the morning?
- Does my child have difficulties following daily routines— anything from dressing in the morning to packing up his school bag?
- Is my child uncoordinated? Does he have trouble with skills such as tying his shoelaces or making his bed?

We never want to put down our kids or make fun of them for these weaknesses. Very likely, there's an underlying disability. The worse they feel about themselves, the more they'll struggle. Children with disabilities can become depressed and develop a defeatist attitude. If this happens, it will be harder than ever to help them overcome their disabilities.

What Causes ADHD?

What causes ADHD? The short answer is that nobody knows for sure, but science has some hunches. Among these are genetics, brain-wiring that's different from the norm, and possible poisons from the environment. Even where genetics are concerned the biological mechanism by which ADHD may be developed is unclear. Is it inherited? Is it a spontaneous genetic dysfunction? The jury is still out. There are suspicions that any or all of the above can impact a child's attention and behavior, though scientists still don't know exactly how any of these lead to ADHD. The best we can say at this point is that ADHD is a symptom that has a variety of possible causes.

One thing we know is that people with ADHD often seem to have brains that are different than those of others. I won't bore you with all the anatomical terminology. Suffice it to say that certain structures in the brain are smaller, show less activity, and receive less blood.

How do we know that the brain is less active? Government research has demonstrated, using PET scans, that individuals with ADHD produce less glucose during activities that require sustained attention. When the brain needs more energy it produces glucose. There is less of this biochemical activity in the brains of those with ADHD. (And no, you should not start feeding your child more sugary foods. The brain doesn't work like that. Cookies will not cure ADHD. Sorry.)

There seem to be genetic factors in ADHD as well. It seems that people can inherit it from their families and if one twin has ADHD it's very likely that the other one has it too.

For those of you who are pregnant or considering becoming pregnant, be warned. There are other possible causes of ADHD. While the evidence is not conclusive, it would be wise to keep away from cigarettes, excessive use of alcohol, and cocaine, as all of these are possible risk factors. Lead in the environment may also be a risk factor. Have your home tested for lead. Even undetectable particles of lead dust settling on surfaces may contribute to ADHD.

There is one substance that has not been proven to cause ADHD—sugar. Despite the persistent myth, there's no evidence that sugar causes hyperactivity or attention deficits of any kind. One reason why this myth may have started is that most children, quite naturally, will get excited when they're in situations where candy is served. If they're at a party and sweets appear, they're likely to become more animated.

It isn't sugar that's the cause; it's just that sugary treats will turn even the best-behaved child into a party animal.

If your child is suspected of having ADHD, there's a series of questions your health care provider will ask. You can ask them yourself. If six or more of the following symptoms (identified by the American Psychiatric Association) have persisted for six months or more, then there is reasonable cause for suspicion. Keep a log and note the dates on which any of these have occurred. Any information you can supply to your child's school or to a health care provider will be most helpful. Ask yourself:

- Does my child make frequent mistakes in schoolwork or other activities due to inattention?
- Does my child lose focus during schoolwork, homework, play, or chores?
- Does my child have poor listening skills?
- Does my child demonstrate poor organizational skills?
- Does my child resist or look for ways to get out of schoolwork and other tasks requiring sustained attention?
- Does my child frequently lose his property?
- Is my child forgetful?
- Is my child easily distractible?

If the evidence is mounting that your child might have ADHD, there are steps to be taken. Some can only be done by a health care provider; others can be done by a health care provider or your child's school. They are as follows.

Medical History

Mom's health during pregnancy will be asked about. It's important, for your child's sake, to be honest. Did you smoke, drink, or use drugs? Any of these could affect your child, so your pediatrician must know about them. Your pediatrician will also examine your child's birth history. Was he underweight or premature? Did he have any medical problems early on?

Your pediatrician will want to know if there were any illnesses during your child's earliest years. Was he injured in any way? Is there any possibility he's been exposed to lead? The better prepared you are to answer these questions, the quicker your child can get all the help to which he's entitled.

The doctor will want to know about your child's emotional life. Is he irritable or does he have a lot of temper tantrums? Does your child have positive or conflicted relationships with other children, teachers (if he's school-aged), or family members?

If your child is in school, bring report cards and scores on achievement tests with you when you visit your pediatrician. If the school has any behavioral reports on your child (sometimes referred to as anecdotal records), get copies and bring them with you to the pediatrician. Also, the doctor will probably ask you if you, your spouse, or any family members have a history of educational or behavior problems. Relax; no one's looking to blame you. (If they are, find another doctor.) All of this information will help to diagnose your child's problems.

Physical Checkup

Your pediatrician will want to know the current state of your child's health. Among the things she'll check for is weight. Not every child has the same height and weight at the same age, but there are ranges of what is considered normal. Your pediatrician will check against a chart to see if your child falls within the normal range or if he's underweight.

Your pediatrician will also examine your child to see if he has any unusual nervous tics or reflex problems. Your child's coordination will also be tested. Again, children have different degrees of coordination. Your doctor's not going to worry whether or not he can hit a home run every time. She'll be more concerned with whether or not your child's coordination falls within the normal range.

Behavioral tests might be administered. There are a variety of professional tests that can be administered by doctors, psychologists, educational evaluators, and classroom teachers. These will help determine whether there's reasonable evidence for a diagnosis of ADHD. There are also a variety of verbal and written tests that help to determine ADHD as well as other learning disabilities. These can be administered by a school psychologist or educational evaluator; or you can ask your pediatrician for a referral for outside testing.

Treatment and Long-Term Management of ADHD

This can be a difficult and scary situation for parents. Treatment can consist of behavior modification, medication, or both. It's hard for any of us to give mental health drugs to our kids. When you're in the process of making the decision, you'll experience conflicting sources of stress. Some friends and relatives will berate you if you even consider medication as an option. They will share every myth and horror story they can dig up.

Others will hint, or even tell you to your face, that you're a bad parent if you don't give your child some sort of medication.

But is it best for them? So what's the best choice? There is no easy answer. This is a decision best made with your immediate family (those who live with you and your child) and your health care provider. Every child is different and will respond to different treatments.

Many parents err on the side of caution and begin with a behavior modification plan, moving to meds only if the plan isn't helping. Others feel their children's condition is so extreme and self-defeating that they might want to try medication as soon as possible. Quite frankly, it's rough living with an impulsive child, no matter how much you love him. In the end, only you can decide the right path.

I can offer two pieces of advice. First, if the choice you make doesn't work out, don't blame. No one can predict for sure the approach that will be best for your child. It's hit or miss. Second, avoid discussing your child's problems with opinionated friends and relatives. They'll only make you confused and they'll do damage to your self-esteem. Your child needs you to be as emotionally resilient as possible. Try to seek out people who will listen and sympathize without offering judgments.

Your pediatrician, your school, or a child psychologist can help you develop and manage a behavioral plan if indeed your child is diagnosed with ADHD. Here are some things the professionals might suggest:

Choose three to five routines that will help your child get through his day. Base the routines on trouble areas. For example, if your child wanders off at the supermarket, one procedure might be that he will always hold on to the cart. The trick is not to tell your child the routine but to go to the store and to actually have him practice it, as if he were learning a part in a play. Arrange several short trips to the store and buy only a few items each time. These are trial runs to practice cart-holding. This method can also be used for talking in our "restaurant voices," packing a book bag, or anything else you deem appropriate. Choose your routines wisely, because if you try more than five of them your child will feel overwhelmed and frustrated.

Remember that old saying "Spare the rod and spoil the child"? Forget it. Children with ADHD and other impairments react badly to physical punishment and to strong verbal reprimands. They'll become agitated, angry, and possibly more resistant than ever. Corporal punishment and verbal abuse often make matters worse. So what's to be done? Remember this simple rule: *Rewards denied are more powerful than punishments received*. Again, keep the punishable behaviors to a minimum, no more than three to five of them. Pick your battles wisely, because if you punish your child for every little thing his behavior will never improve. Conduct ongoing conversations with your child about your behavioral rules. Remind him that if he does *A*, he will lose *B*.

Along with punishments, small rewards can be powerful tools for improving the behavior of an ADHD child. Put up a chart on your refrigerator. If your child completes a predetermined task each day, such as brushing his teeth or packing his schoolbag, put a check on the chart or some sort of cute sticker. Decide in advance what the reward will be and which behaviors will earn rewards.

Keep it simple. For example, five checks might equal one hour of TV time watching Saturday morning cartoons. Five smiley face stickers might equal pizza for dinner on Friday night. That's the stuff rewards are made of. Don't offer money or hundred-dollar sneakers or a trip with ten friends to the movies. Behavior management shouldn't put you in debt.

Work with your child's teacher to set her own system of rewards and punishments. Calling out in class might result in ten-minutes detention while other children are at recess. Punishments don't have to be severe to be effective. They do have to be consistent, though. A school reward can be as simple as a cute sticker at the end of the day for not calling out. Again, the size of the reward isn't as important as the consistency of its application.

Medicating a Child with ADHD

You may feel pressure to medicate your child, and it may or may not be a good option for your child. Speak to your doctor about medications. Most medications used to treat ADHD are, oddly enough, stimulants. They would make an adult more hyper, but in children they have the opposite effect.

The biggest area of concern with stimulants is that they turn some children into "zombies," unaware of the world around them and unresponsive. Fortunately, this is a temporary condition that can be altered with a change of dosage or by trying a different medication. Your doctor should be quickly informed if there are any such problems.

There are new drugs on the market, some of which are not stimulants. Make sure your doctor takes the time to explore the wide variety of options now available. If your pediatrician or child psychiatrist doesn't allow plenty of time for questions or discussion, my advice is to find someone who will. No matter how you slice it, medication is an anxiety-inducing option and your doctor should give you all the time you need to understand your medicinal options.

If stimulants aren't sufficient, your pediatrician might suggest combining the medication with an antidepressant. Generally, your doctor will begin treatment with the lowest dosage of a stimulant or antidepressant. If it doesn't help, then the dosage will be increased. In time, you might have to try different medications or combinations of drugs.

Hang in there. For many children with ADHD, treatment does help. Unfortunately, there are no guarantees, but many families have experienced happy results. Remember, the medication will often be combined with behavior therapy. So if meds are prescribed, you and your child's teacher will still have work ahead of you.

Depression

Depression and anxiety aren't learning disabilities per se, but experts recognize that they interfere with a child's ability to learn, concentrate, and remember information. It's vital that families recognize the symptoms of depression and seek help as soon as possible. Depression is sometimes hard to recognize in children because they're not as skilled as adults at expressing their feelings.

Additionally, some of the symptoms of childhood depression are obvious but others might surprise you. Aggressive behaviors in some children might in fact be symptoms of depression. Other symptoms of depression are internal and may be harder to ferret out.

It's also important to note that not all episodes of sadness are symptoms of depression. Depression is an illness that lasts for a long period of time. It is marked by a lack of resiliency that other children might have after traumatic events occur. To confuse things even further, not all episodes of depression are the results of obvious traumas.

Depression can be caused by anything from stress at school to parental divorce. There's also evidence that the tendency toward depression can be inherited in many cases. When depression runs in families, the sufferers often have abnormal levels of various brain chemicals. This condition is often referred to as a chemical imbalance.

Following is a series of questions you can ask yourself. If the answer to one or more of these is yes and if your child has displayed these symptoms for two weeks or more, then it's time to consult a health care professional.

- Is my child often irritable? Does she get angry at the drop of a hat?
- Does my child react strongly to rejection or to imagined rejection from others?
- Does my child cry easily and often?
- Does my child suffer from separation anxiety? Is she excessively "clingy"?
- Has my child become withdrawn? Does she spend a lot of time alone, avoiding the company of others, including peers?

- Does my child have frequent headaches or stomach aches? Has a medical checkup ruled out any obvious causes?
- Does my child put herself down?
- Does my child sleep way too much or, conversely, wake up throughout the night? Does she have frequent difficulty getting out of bed?
- Has my child had a change in appetite, either eating too much or losing weight because she's eating too little?
- Has my child lost interest in activities that she once enjoyed?

If any of these symptoms have gone on for some time, there's cause for concern. Get help and don't assume "she'll grow out of it." Depressed people cannot learn, cannot read well, and cannot think well. Long-term depression can have deleterious effects on intellectual growth. Depression can also be the precursor to other troubles such as bipolar disorder or suicidal tendencies.

If your child is diagnosed with depression, there are several options. Discuss these with your health care provider. It couldn't hurt to get a second opinion, either.

- **Cognitive therapy:** Your child will be taught to recognize negative thoughts and to notice how her thoughts influence her feelings and behavior. Cognitive therapy involves learning to challenge negative thoughts that are exaggerated or not based on reality.
- **Behavioral therapy:** While cognitive therapy focuses on thoughts and feelings, behavioral therapy focuses on actions. In this approach, negative behaviors are changed by confronting feared objects and situations over and over until they lose their power to intimidate. This is sometimes referred to as desensitizing the patient. Behavioral therapy may include relaxation techniques to increase your child's level of desensitization. Many mental health practitioners combine elements of cognitive and behavioral therapy.

- **Social skills therapy:** Many depressed children (and adults) feel powerless over their environments. Social skills therapy helps change that perception by teaching specific skills such as starting a conversation, joining in on activities in a way that's assertive but not aggressive, or learning how to stand up for oneself by saying "no" in a manner that is firm but not combative.
- **Medication:** There are a variety of medications that alter brain chemicals. In the past few years, there has been a dramatic increase in prescriptions for children. With this increase has come an increase in accusations that some drugs worsen the thoughts and behavior of depressed children. If your health care provider recommends medication, engage him in a frank discussion about the risks and potential benefits. Make sure that you and your physician have a plan in place for monitoring your child's response to any antidepressant that is prescribed. Also, ask if your child should receive some form of therapy in conjunction with medication. This is the approach taken by many clinicians.

Bipolar Disorder

Bipolar disorder, as its name implies, has two behavioral poles or extremes. One is the high-energy pole, or mania. The other is the depressive pole. There may be moments in between when a bipolar child appears more balanced, but then the mood swings begin again. Bipolar disorder is not something your child's school can treat. You must seek medical help, and fast.

Left untreated, bipolar disorder is quite dangerous. Disruption to a child's education is the least of it. Even very young children can become so exhausted by the emotional swings that make up this disorder that they seek relief in suicide. Bipolar children should be taken seriously if they threaten to harm themselves or if they express feelings of low self-worth.

Following are two sets of questions to help you determine whether your child may be suffering from bipolar disorder. Remember, if your child is bipolar, you will answer yes to some of the questions on each list.

The Manic Pole:

- Does my child at times have a dramatic increase in energy or restlessness?
- Does my child sometimes seem euphoric or "silly" beyond what circumstances call for?
- Does my child begin talking very fast? Do his conversations (or more likely his monologues) leap from one topic to another and another?
- Does my child have a tough time focusing on tasks or conversations?
- Does he sleep poorly and yet wake up "bouncing off the walls"?
- Does my child engage in socially or even sexually inappropriate activities?
- Does my child "leap before he looks"? Does he put himself into situations that endanger him or others without weighing the consequences?
- Has my child developed an overinflated ego, believing he can do things beyond his age or capabilities?

The Depressive Pole:

- Does my child express feelings of hopelessness or worthlessness?
- Is my child fatalistic? Does he feel he has no control when bad things happen in the world or inside himself?
- Does my child become irritated or angry with little provocation?
- Does my child sleep either poorly or way too much?
- Is there a sharp change in my child's appetite accompanied by sudden weight loss or weight gain?
- Has my child lost interest in activities he once enjoyed?
- Has my child become hypersensitive to criticism? Does any type of disappointment or rejection get him extremely upset?
- Does my child talk of suicide, death, or the end of the world?
- Has my child made a suicide attempt?

Treatment of Bipolar Disorder

Since this is an extreme disorder, if you suspect that your child is bipolar, find a mental health practitioner who specializes in working with children. Inquire into the clinician's experience working with bipolar kids. As with other disorders, your health care provider will probably suggest some combination of medication and therapy. Again, be sure that your doctor provides you with a plan to monitor your child's progress and advises you of a plan of action in case of a crisis. Take this disorder seriously, but be comforted that many children have been helped. There are no guarantees, but treatment certainly raises your child's odds of improving.

Asperger's Syndrome

This neurological disorder (some call it a mild form of autism, others a nonverbal learning disability) is at once a curse and a blessing. Children with Asperger's syndrome can experience troubling social problems, yet they can grow up to be highly successful and creative individuals. Some of history's eccentric geniuses likely had this puzzling mental quirk.

Children with Asperger's syndrome process social relationships in peculiar ways. Intellectually, they're normal. Artistically, they're often stand-outs; but socially they go bust, often being teased or ostracized because of the peculiar things they say and do.

Here are some questions you can ask that might clue you in to whether your child has Asperger's syndrome:

- Does my child say weird things that come out of left field?
- Does my child get upset or even throw tantrums if her routine has changed or if she is placed in new social settings, no matter how harmless those settings appear to be?
- Does my child seem oblivious to nonverbal cues from other people? Is she shocked when people get angry or insulted by some of the things she says?
- Does my child "invade other people's space" and seem oblivious when others show signs of discomfort?
- Does my child have a special skill or talent that is unusually developed for a person of her age?

- Does my child have a "subject" or area of interest about which she is obsessed? Does she talk about her subject incessantly at inappropriate times and in inappropriate places?
- Though she speaks grammatically, does my child have an odd cadence to her speech that makes her sound peculiar?
- Does my child seem like a junior Einstein one minute and a social disaster the next?

Treating Asperger's Syndrome

There are no treatments that are exclusive to Asperger's syndrome, but some of the following might be suggested by your mental health practitioner:

- Behavioral therapy
- Social skills therapy
- Educational supports as needed
- Education about the disorder for family members

As with other disorders, medication might be prescribed. Discuss the pros and cons with your clinician. Make sure you are educated on potential side effects. As always, you are your child's best advocate.

The most important bit of advice I can offer is to remember that life is unpredictable. We cannot predetermine who our children will become. Whatever their challenges and eccentricities, the best thing we can do is manage our own emotions and love our children for who they are. A calm and loving adult is the best thing for a child, no matter what their life circumstances may be.

Conclusion

Throughout recorded history, literacy has been the ticket to success. Ancient scholars and scribes were revered and were offered opportunities afforded to few in their societies. The same holds true today. Strong reading and writing skills are the fundamentals of a good education. Without these, other subjects cannot be learned with any depth. Well-read and articulate people get the best jobs and the greatest chances to achieve economic success. Literate people compel the respect of their societies. Even those who rebel against society are more likely to succeed if they're well read and capable of communicating their ideas to others.

Literacy goes hand-in-hand with critical thinking. The more you read about other people, experiences, and diverse ideas, the more likely you are to develop a keen mind. Literate folks have the training to make careful judgments about politics, social issues, and the challenges of everyday life. If we want our children to become adults who live well, they must learn to read and think well.

But beyond all the external successes, the internal ones remain the most compelling: the moments of excitement, suspense, wonderment, mystery, humor, and pathos that come from reading books. Reading is nothing less than one of life's great thrills and all children (and adults of course) should have their minds and souls opened to the infinite pleasures to be found in literature.

Index

About the Author

Hal W. Lanse, PhD, is a longtime teacher trainer living and working in New York City. He has collaborated with several schools on improving their instructional programs. Known for his engaging, interactive training workshops, Dr. Lanse has addressed topics ranging from family literacy to behavior management. As a single, adoptive parent, he is aware and deeply concerned about the educational needs of families. You can sign up for Hal Lanse's monthly education newsletter for parents and teachers at *www.readwellthinkwell.com.*